IS 1988

FISHERMEN'S CONFLICT

John Corin

The story of a Cornish fishing port

I curry not with smoothing terms,
Ne yet rude threats I blast:
I seek no patron for my faults,
I plead no needless haste.
(From Richard Carew's preface to his *Survey of Cornwall*, 1602)

Tops'l Books

Published 1988 by
Tops'l Books
(an imprint of David & Charles)
Newton Abbot London North Pomfret (Vt)

© **1988 John Corin**

British Library Cataloguing in Publication Data

Corin, John
Fisherman's conflict : the story of a
Cornish fishing port.
1. Fisheries – England – Penzance
(Cornwall) – History 2. Newlyn
(Penzance, Cornwall) – Social life and
customs 3. Penzance (Cornwall) –
Social life and customs
I. Title
942.3'75 DA690.P4

ISBN 0 7153 9107 0

All rights reserved. No part of this publication may
be reproduced, stored in a retrieval system, or
transmitted in any form or by any means, electronic,
mechanical, photocopying, recording or otherwise,
with the prior permission of David & Charles
Publishers plc

Photoset and printed in Great Britain
by Redwood Burn Ltd, Trowbridge, Wilts
for David & Charles Publishers plc
Brunel House Newton Abbot Devon

Cover picture

A serious-looking group of Newlyn men, with a fish jouster's cart, gathered at the Old Harbour in Newlyn, before the building of the North Pier. In the background are gaff-rigged East Anglian fishing vessels, competitors in the mackerel fishery, whose presence gave rise to the incidents described in this book. (*Photo: Reg Watkis collection*)

By the same author

Provident and the Story
of the Brixham Smacks

Penlee Lifeboat
(with Grahame Farr)

Sennen Cove and
its Lifeboat

Contents

Acknowledgements

I am indebted to Ben Batten, a Newlyn Town man born and bred, for reading the typescript and making a number of suggestions, and above all for his encouragement. He very kindly made available to me Janie Kelynack's invaluable manuscript memoirs of Newlyn in the last century. Ben Batten has published several studies of Newlyn's past and is a follower of the motto from the Federation of Old Cornwall Societies, *Kyntelleugh an brewyon es gesys na vo kellys travyth*, 'Gather up the fragments that remain, that nothing be lost' (John 6:12.)

Mrs. Blanche Brown also very kindly made available to me her memoirs of Newlyn in her youth. David Butcher of Lowestoft, who writes on the East Anglian fishery, generously supplied research on the subject of the Newlyn Riots from his sources.

Andrew Munson, Harbour Master at Newlyn, and Broundand Tonkin, Sea Fisheries officer for Cornwall County Council have been most helpful at various stages and also read the typescript and made suggestions. Any remaining errors and omissions are the sole responsibility of the author.

Tony Pawlyn, a Newlyn man and chairman of the South West Maritime History Society has kindly given encouragement and advice all the way along and I am indebted to him and many others for information and the use of photographs, in particular Miss Emily Bath, Miss Margaret Bazeley, Clive Carter, Peter Garnier, Frank Gibson, Ronald Harvey, Morgan Hosking, Del Johnson, John Laity, Mrs. Rene Nash, Clifton Pender and the Pender family in Mousehole, Mrs. Marjorie Phillips, Peter Pool, Dr. Eric Richards, Miss Hilda May Richards, William Richards, William Stevenson, Reg Watkiss, Douglas Williams, Jack Worth, and the staffs of the Penzance Library in the Morrab Gardens, Redruth County Library, and the Royal Institution of Cornwall.

J. M. Dent & Sons Ltd kindly gave permission for the quotation of the passages from Charles Lee's *The Widow Woman* on pages 59 and 63 and William Kimber kindly gave permission for the quotation on page 51 from Leo Tregenza's *Harbour Village*.

Last, but not by any means least, I must acknowledge the contribution of my editor Colin Elliott, from whose idea this book sprang.

J.C.

A crew of Newlyn fishermen in the days of sail (*Photo: Reg Watkis collection*)

CHAPTER ONE

Send A Gunboat!

No man claims an acre of ocean as his own

(W. S. Lach-Szyrma)

'Send a gunboat', we are led to believe, was a standard injunction in British foreign policy in the great days of Empire. The treatment was normally confined to those whom Kipling described as 'lesser breeds without the Law'. In Western Europe more discreet diplomatic methods were the rule. Nevertheless when violence erupted in a fishing village on the Celtic fringe of the United Kingdom in May 1896, the government of Lord Salisbury promptly sent not one gunboat but three and followed up with the despatch of three hundred redcoats of the Royal Berkshire Regiment.

The trouble was at the Cornish port of Newlyn where riots broke out on the morning of Monday, May 18th, 1896, and the cause was a quarrel between the local fishermen and 'foreigners' from East Anglia over the matter of Sunday Observance! The Cornishmen were in the main staunch chapel goers and did not go to sea on Sundays. The east coast men, or 'Yorkies', as they were somewhat inaccurately known as they come from Suffolk, had no inhibition about fishing on the Sabbath.

There had been clashes over this issue some twenty years previously, at St. Ives in 1876 and at Scilly in 1877. Indeed St. Ives had a bye-law forbidding fishing on a Sunday. Only a few Cornish fishermen now observe the Sunday rule, although in February 1983 the district council still voted against Sunday pleasureboat operation at St. Ives. In the nineteenth century the ports on the west coast of the United Kingdom, including the Isle of Man, and those in Ireland, maintained the rule on Sunday fishing against all comers.

The religious devotion of the Cornish fishermen was undoubted. It was customary on commencing to shoot the nets to say the words 'In the Name of the Lord'. There was also a prayer on leaving port,

'Safe out, safe in and a blessing'.

Some were more devout than others. James Henry Treloar Cliff, who became coxswain of the Porthoustock Lifeboat, records in his memoirs that in about 1892 he joined the Porthleven fishing boat *Emblem* for the Scottish herring fishery. They had a fair wind all the way up the Channel, but on coming abreast of Dover it was declared that as the morrow was Sunday they would put in and go to chapel. Cliff was a Church of England man and it was his only experience of missing a fair wind to go to chapel.

In the latter part of the last century, Scilly was much used as a base for the mackerel fishing season by Newlyn and East Anglian men. On a Sunday evening the Newlyn men would assemble in hollow squares on The Parade in Hugh Town and sing Methodist hymns in rich and moving harmonies. 'Let's 'ave 'em soft, then give 'em lip' the conductor would say.

Some, of course, were less devout. Commercial fishing then, and now, is a hard life, and a hard life does not necessarily produce angels. There was a rougher element present and hundreds of active young men kept in port by bad weather were liable to misbehave. In June 1883 *The Cornishman* reported that 'For fourpence about 300 hobble-de-hoys, mostly employed in fishing (for the sake of the good name of the villages where they reside, we will not mention the names of the places) are allowed every Sunday evening to defile the floors of the gallery of the Salvation Army, Fort Herbert, with orange peel, expectoration from chewing tobacco etc., in addition to annoying persons underneath, with their abominable, ignorant, ill-mannered and disgusting behaviour'. The newspaper went on to report indignantly that on a recent Sunday evening the collecting box from one gallery contained only 1½d (½p) and from another 2½d (1p).

So, in a generally stable, well-ordered, God-fearing community of hard working people there were those capable of mob violence on that May morning. In the terms of the Riot Act they only had 'to alarm at least one person of reasonable firmness and courage'. By swarming on to the east coast boats, throwing 100,000 mackerel overboard and in later skirmishes and a pitched battle they certain alarmed many.

The reaction of the authorities was predictable on the basis of past performances. Only three years previously soldiers had fired on unarmed Yorkshire miners at Featherstone, who were protesting about wage cuts. In the Gordon Riots of 1780 there were 285 people killed. Over the period 1730–1840, in the course of riots, 495 were killed by the authorities, 5 by the rioters and 91 were subsequently executed. It all gave some justification for the American Mr. Bierce's sardonic comment, that riots are a popular entertainment given to the military by innocent bystanders. Admittedly the sternness of the authorities and the tendency to over-react in a reckless manner had somewhat moderated by the end of the Victorian era, but by modern standards the sending of so many troops and warships seems to be a remarkable over-reaction. One reason was that the civil power, now entirely relied on in all but the gravest emergencies, was then much weaker. There were only 219 policemen in the whole of Cornwall, or one to every 1,356 inhabitants. The neighbouring Penzance borough force, at that time a separate entity whose jurisdiction did not extend to Newlyn, numbered 13. Apart from the time it would have taken to assemble, an effective force would have denuded the rest of the county of police cover. There are currently some 720 police in Cornwall, or one to every 600 inhabitants, and it is still regarded as being under strength.

If the operational reaction to the riots was stern the subsequent judicial re-action was extraordinarily mild. When a handful of rioters were eventually hauled before the Judge of Assize they were let off with the kind of mild admonition for which modern benches are often criticised. So, evidently, the present day impression that all Victorian society was well-behaved, that everyone went to church or chapel and respected the Sabbath, and that swift retribution and exemplary punishment followed all wrong-doing needs some revision in the light of the Newlyn Riots.

Shakespeare's Richard II remarks that 'Rash fierce blaze of riot cannot last'. By the Thursday matters had cooled down in Newlyn. Of themselves the riots were not of great significance. Despite a great deal of sound and fury there were no deaths, no significant casualties reported and, by modern standards, damage to property was minimal. They were possibly less dangerous than a modern football riot. The fishermen's action and their subsequent wordy protests achieved nothing and the action was never repeated. Neverthless it marked the beginning of the end of an era and raises a number of questions relevant to the social and industrial development of this part of Cornwall. They are questions which, as we shall see, are not without significance to the Cornish fishing industry to-day.

What was such a large and competitive east coast fleet doing in the west? What was the attraction? How had tiny Newlyn become big enough to contain it and provide it with access to the markets? Was religious feeling at the time really strong enough to spark off so much trouble over the observance of the Fourth Commandment? Or was that only an excuse for the Cornishmen to protest against the presence of strangers in their waters?

What sort of society was it which produced such a brief and isolated flare up of violence in a peaceful Cornish bay? Nearly a century later could such a thing possibly happen again?

Sporadic conflict has been a feature of commercial fishing in many places from time immemorial, due to the fact that the fisherman is both a nomad and a hunter. To those not well acquainted with the industry it may appear that a fishing fleet goes out from its base port to a ground, near or far, and returns home to market its catch. This may too often be the pattern, but is very far from being the regular rule. Particularly in the last century fleets followed different species of fish from season to season around the entire coasts of the British Isles. They might thus be away from their home port, catching fish and landing it at any convenient market for a large part of the year.

A century ago the Vicar of Newlyn, the Reverend Wladislaw Lach-Szyrma, commented that no man claimed an acre of ocean as his own. Nations might claim narrow strips of territorial water, but no fishermen or group of fishermen had rights to any fishing grounds in the sense that a farmer owns or tenants his fields. Competition can come from the next cove, the next port, another county or distant country. An extreme example of the wide-ranging nature of fishing was provided by the sperm whalers. British and American whalers cruised over all the oceans of the world in their search for catches competing against each other and men from other nations too.

Conflict not only arose over the catching of particular species of fish in their season on a same grounds. Different methods of fishing for the same species, or different species, in the same sea area were also a source of friction. Trawling has been unpopular with practitioners of other methods for at least six hundred years. In 1376 a conservation lobby petitioned Parliament to ban the small mesh size used in trawls and complained bitterly that the small fish caught only went for animal food. They asked for remedy and perhaps they got it in some measure. At least the word which was then used for a trawl net, *wondyrchoum*, was replaced by the modern monosyllable, of obscure origin. Maybe it comes from the Middle Dutch word *traghelen*, 'to drag'. Following a further move by the conservation lobby in the time of Charles the First, the king took 'into consideration the great destruction made of fish by a net or engine now called the Trawle'.

Fish became a source of conflict both locally and nationally in the Middle Ages. Hastings men had many bitter quarrels with Yarmouth men at Yarmouth. The Scots tried to keep everybody out of their coastal waters, while the Norwegians and later the Danes had troubles in Iceland, where they had sovereignty. In the medieval diet meat was so scarce in winter, because of the primitive agricultural economy, that fish were a most important source of protein. It might almost be said that cod and herring held the same place in the international scene as oil does today. At a very early date there was trouble over the English desire to obtain cod from Iceland. Bristol merchants took out general goods to Iceland and in return brought cod, hake, pollack, salmon and herring. Trading was under licence from the Danish King, but the English were troublesome, and probably greedy. They slew the Governor of Iceland in a riot and the licences were withdrawn. As a consequence they turned westward in the North Atlantic to find their own cod on the Banks of Newfoundland. The expeditions were the background to the discovery of the North American mainland in 1497, causing the historian Fuller to say of the English adventurers, 'When going to fish for cod, they have found a country.' In our own times the quarrel with Iceland erupted again with the so called Cod Wars, ending in the disastrous rout of British fishing from Icelandic waters.

Around the British Isles there was surprisingly a general tolerance. Indeed, in writing of Yorkshire, Camden was moved to remark 'The English always granted leave for fishing, reserving the honours to themselves, but, out of lazy humour, resigning the gains to others'. It is a tendency which now seems to live on in the sphere of British inventions. But basically the Newlyn vicar's comment about no man owning an acre of ocean held good. After the Middle

Ages there was not much serious national rivalry over fishing. As all enterprising groups of fishermen went further afield into each other's home waters there was a feeling of 'Live and let live' and the mingling was beneficial in the spread of improved techniques. The Dutch were leaders. Even such a local Cornish word as *balking house* for the huer's hut, from which look out was kept for the appearance of a shoal, could be derived froma the Dutch word, *balken*, to cry out.

There was in previous centuries no real pressure on stocks of fish like herring and cod. The shoals appeared inexhaustible, as indeed they were in relation to the total catches of the time. But even in 1881 an expert observer de Caux, warned: 'The stern fact is, that the sea *is* exhaustible'. But in the nineteenth century fishing was very much a free-for-all and with seemingly plenty for all conflict was limited, compared with either the Middle Ages or to-day. Nevertheless a combination of geography and history could make a particular port vulnerable to competition in its home waters and this proved to be the case with Newlyn.

In the middle ground the Keel Alley area of Newlyn about a century ago. The prominent house with the portico top left is Antoine House. Otherwise the scene bears little resemblance to that of to-day, with extensive harbour development taking place in the foreground, commencing in 1987, following a first phase completed in 1980. (*Photo: Alfred Robinson*)

CHAPTER TWO

The Growth Of A Port

Hes Coornwall a nashion, hes a a Hiland,
or hes a a furren country?
He hedn't no nashion, he hedn't no highlan,
nor he hedn't no ferren country.
What hes a then?
Why he's kidged to a furren country from the top hand.
(School Dame Peggy Combellack's geography question, quoted in A. K. Hamilton-Jenkin's *The Cornish Miner*.)

The situation of Newlyn as a fishing port has certain similarities with that of its Devon neighbour Brixham, which has pursued a different fishing tradition becoming noted as a trawler port. Neither had the advantage of a good natural harbour, but both are tucked into a corner of a large bay with protection from prevailing westerly winds and the gales they bring. Newlyn lies in the north-west extremity of Mount's Bay adjacent to the part of the bay known, somewhat confusingly, as Gwavas Lake, although it is not a lake.

The thirteenth edition of the Admiralty Pilot for the South Coast says: 'Mount's Bay affords anchorage in several places, according to the wind, but Gwavas Lake and Penzance Bay, on the western shore, are the best; they are sheltered from all winds except those between south south west and south east, which send in a heavy sea, against which few vessels could ride with any prospect of success were it not for the powerful undertow, the resistance of which increases with the strength and duration of the wind, thus enabling them to ride more easily. In the winter season, however, Mount's Bay should not be used except as a temporary anchorage before entering one of the harbours'. The Admiralty Pilot is not normally noted for its optimism about any conditions, but any mariner anchored in Mount's Bay in a southerly gale would probably regard the assistance of the undertow as a rather dubious theoretical benefit.

Like Torbay, on which Brixham stands, Mount's Bay has the considerable advantage that sailing vessels can enter and leave it in almost any wind direction and do not have to contend with a strong tidal stream in the approaches. Thus fishing vessels would rarely be wind-bound in port, or unable to land their catches. Both Newlyn and Brixham have, in modern times, developed large artificial harbours to compensate for the otherwise rather meagre natural advantages. At Newlyn the entrance to the harbour faces north east towards the opposite shore of Mount's Bay, so that even in a gale from that quarter there is little fetch in the seas, while the land extending to Penlee Point to the south affords the shelter from westerly winds. It is claimed that the entrance to the harbour, locally known as 'The Gaps', has never been closed through stress of weather.

However, Newlyn's principal geographical advantage lay in its position in relation to fishing grounds, both near and far. Almost at the tip of south west Britain, in fact but a few miles from Land's End, there was a choice of access to waters on both the west and east coasts of Britain and the southerly situation put Newlyn well within the limits of the pilchard shoals. The pilchard being a warm water fish has seldom in recent times been taken east of Dartmouth and in even more recent times the limit has been a little east of Plymouth. The season for pilchards was late summer and autumn.

When the corn is in the shock,
Then the fish are on the rock.

The other principal fish shoaling locally were the mackerel and the season for them was winter and spring. The end of the season came after Easter. It used to be said, 'Balaam and Balak were read in the lesson to-day. No more fish now, the mackerel season is over'. The story of Balaam and the ass which answered him back, Numbers 22, is appointed for the third Sunday after Easter. From 1870 the Newlyn men were able to use Scilly as a base and fish the mackerel ground 25 to 30 miles north west of the Land's End. A certain amount of mackerel was also taken by inshore seining in the summer.

Newlyn also has the advantage of being near the northern limit of warm water fish and near the southern limit of cold water fish.

From at least as early as 1826 the Newlyn men began to fill the gap between spring and late summer by reaching out for the herring in Irish waters at the end of May and into June and late July. In 1882 however they did not go, as an expression of their feelings over the Irish outrages in Britain. By 1847 they were going up the English Channel for the great autumn fishery of the herring off Yorkshire and East Anglia, also some to the Manx ports and to Kinsale in October for winter mackerel. But generally speaking it was the custom to return to Newlyn by the beginning of October for Paul Feast. This is the patronal festival of the parish church of St. Pol-de-Leon, a major event in the local calendar.

By the eighties and nineties Newlyn boats were circumnavigating the British Isles in the cycle of the fishing seasons, some going as far as Shetland, others making use of the Caledonian Canal. Their navigational aids were minimal by modern standards. At that time it was the policy of the Royal National Lifeboat Institution to supply barometers to fishermen at a subsidised price of about 13s. (65p) and also to provide public ones ashore.

The only navigational instruments the Newlyn boats carried would have been a compass, of doubtful deviation, an hour glass and a lead line. The bellows for the cabin stove provided a surface on which a traverse board was improvised. They maintained a constant sub-conscious sense of their whereabouts. In the Second World War a navigational specialist in an armed trawler found that the Brixham man aboard could always give a rough position without apparently doing any navigational work at all.

In the absence of weather forecasts keen observation of the sky, the behaviour of sea-birds, marine life and even the colour of the rust on a buoy were the only insurance against being caught-out. Losses of Newlyn boats seem to have been rare although there were casualties on board from time to time.

But while the Newlyn men ranged the British seas in the first half of the nineteenth century their home port remained of only local importance. Its harbour, enclosed by a single medieval quay, provided only a small area of berthage, which dried out. The home market for fish caught off west Cornwall and landed in Mount's Bay was purely local and confined to the small population of the peninsula. London was 300 miles away and Bristol 200. If they were fishing up the English Channel or Bristol Channel the Newlyn boats might land direct to Plymouth, Weymouth, Southampton, Portsmouth, Cardiff, or Swansea. If they were far out at sea they formed companies of about nine boats, sending one boat to market each day. Alternatively fast cutters acting as market boats went from Mount's Bay to Portsmouth, Bristol and Swansea. During Lent horse-drawn transport was used to some extent to take fish to the big centres of population. From East Anglia it was the regular means of getting fish to Billingsgate. The fish must have been rather less than fresh on arrival, despite a liberal use of salt!

In short, Newlyn was developing an important fishing fleet, but, even with the arrival of railways in Cornwall, lacked any satisfactory means of marketing fish landed there anywhere outside the county. However, in 1859 there took place an event which eventually transformed the face of Cornwall. The Royal Albert Bridge at Saltash, Brunel's masterpiece, was completed. Cornwall's isolated railways were connected to the national system, and the last English county to be connected. The Cornish peninsula was no longer almost an island. The effect of the rail connection on the economic and social life of the county as a whole can hardly be exaggerated. Newlyn lay a little way beyond the terminus at Penzance, but effectively the small fishing port was now rail-connected and a new era began.

Railway development in Cornwall began in the first quarter of the 19th century. The main impetus came from the requirements of the mineral industry. What later became part of the main line through Cornwall, the section from Penzance to Truro, the West Cornwall Railway, was completed by 1852. But the section from Truro to Saltash, the Cornwall Railway, was not opened until 1859, the year of the completion of the Royal Albert Bridge at Saltash. Eventually all the railways in Cornwall which survived came under the aegis of the Great Western Railway, with the exception of the lines from Launceston to Padstow, Bodmin to Wadebridge, and from Devon to Bude, which came under the London & South Western Railway, later the Southern. The line from Saltash to Penzance remained the main railway artery, as it is to-day.

The opening of the railway link between Cornwall and the rest of the country in May 1859 was beyond question the most important single event in the history of Cornwall in modern times. Nothing quite so significant had happened since the arrival of the Saxon King Athelstan in 927 A.D. Then, according to tradition, Athelstan's army finally overcame King Howal and the Cornish resistance fighters at Boleit, a little way to the west of Newlyn. The authority of the English crown was thus imposed on Cornwall by conquest, with all that that legally implied, but Cornwall continued socially and economically much in its own way until the invasion by railway nearly a millenium later. The second invasion had far more profound effects which are still working themselves out today.

In its way Cornwall was in the forefront of the Industrial Revolution. The very absence of a railway connection and other than expensive sea-borne coal supplies positively encouraged the development of the steam engine, with Richard Trevithick as the outstanding pioneer, using high pressure steam, as opposed to Watt's low pressure engines. The cost of pumping water from the tin mines by steam engine encouraged the invention of more conomical engines. From the demand for those engines sprang the associated foundries of the county which in their time achieved great distinction. The immediate effect of the railway was to provide a more economical and safer route for the county's imports of fuel and raw materials. In the case of exports, mineral products benefited immediately, but a considerable period elapsed before Cornish agriculture developed a surplus of products like broccoli and flowers for export. On the other hand the fishing industry with its highly perishable product was in a position to start generating a surplus and sending it to up-country markets immediately.

The arrival of the railway was hailed by Mr. G. Smith, Chairman of the West Cornwall Railway, speaking at the celebration in Truro on May 3rd, 1859: 'The title of one of our Kings was King of England with Cornwall and from the days of Richard the Third to the present Cornwall has been presumed to hold a sort of Berwick-on-Tweed position, neither within nor without the borders – but now we are part of England' (cheers).

Twelve years before, the Vicar of Bodmin, the Rev. John Wallis, compiling The Cornwall Register, had taken a prescient view:

'When the railways have brought Plymouth, the Tamar and the whole of Cornwall within a journey of twelve (!) hours from London, no part of the United Kingdom will be more frequently or constantly explored.'

On May 6th, 1859, the *Royal Cornwall Gazette* was already looking at the scenic aspects of the line and contrasting the view of Cornwall given by the main road with that of the railway route, in favour of the latter:

'Ever charming, ever new,
When will the landscape tire the view!'

The Devil features quite frequently in Cornish folk-lore but according to a somewhat inconsistent tradition he never entered into Cornwall for fear of being put into a pasty. There are those who hold that he overcame this fear in 1859 and came in over the Royal Albert Bridge at Saltash, with the railway. He was followed by a growing horde of Englishmen, greater by far than Athelstan's army, who have now come to outnumber the native inhabitants, with a concomitant social and cultural effect. While initially the railway gave impetus to the industrial development of Cornwall it also made possible the great annual flood of the tourist trade which was to come. In the end the county which was one of the first to be industrialised became one of the first to be de-industrialised; even to the extent that now any industrial development which might be deemed to affect the tourists' enjoyment is looked at askance. Indeed objectors often include residents who have come from outside the county who do not wish to see industry on the landscape.

Down in Mount's Bay the massive Queen's Hotel was completed on the Promenade at Penzance in 1862 followed by the Mount's Bay Hotel and the prosperous houses of Alexandra Road. And in 1866 there came an early omen of future attitudes when Penzance Town Council sought to ban Newlyn fishermen from drying their nets on the beach in front of the hotel. However, serious thoughts of de-industrialisation lay far in the future. The immediate effect on Newlyn of the rail connection was to give the fishermen the up-country market which had previously been denied them.

Newlyn itself at this stage could scarcely be called a fishing port, but rather a fishing community, boasting only a small medieval quay, enclosing a drying harbour which a score or so of boats would fill. It had to look to the railway terminus at Penzance to send away the fish which it landed, but it was not slow to grasp the opportunity and indeed to extend it. There were good mackerel grounds to the west of Scilly, but the distance made it difficult for the sailing luggers to land the fish on the mainland in good condition. By about 1867 however the practice of what was in effect *klondyking* had been started. This term means the direct shipping of fish from a port rather than landing it for local sale and marketing. It has been much used in recent years in relation to the Eastern bloc vessels which have been loading the mackerel catches made off south west of England and the west of Scotland, but the term is an old one, born at the time when a boom in herring being shipped to the Continent coincided with the famous Klondyke gold rush.

The Newlyn men began to make use of the regular steamer connection established between St. Mary's, Scilly and Penzance to get their fish to the mainland from whence they were shipped in.

Even today, when government and industry make use of all the techniques of economic planning in an attempt to forecast the long term effect of any development, major changes in the pattern of activity frequently has consequences which are not wholly anticipated. The gaining of access to a distant market by the Newlyn men as a result of the railway had consequences which certainly proved far reaching and not altogether those predicted. We have seen that by 1826 the Newlyn men were going as far as Ireland and by the middle of the century to northern British waters. If they could fish far from their home port, so could other men from distant parts of Britain, particularly those skilled in drift-net fishing.

It may be assumed that the Newlyn men were not slow to begin using the railway at Penzance to send away fish. In the first half of 1861 the railway carried 1,063 tons of fish in Cornwall and in the following year there was a thirty percent increase in the same period. It has been suggested that one unlooked for consequence of up-country marketing was the decline in the catching of cheaper fish – the staple of the poor. Whether the Newlyn men anticipated that fishermen from Brixham and the east coast of England would begin using Mount's Bay as a base and a landing port we cannot know. Certainly in later years, when the question of building a very large harbour at Newlyn arose, the older fishermen perceived that what was good for the local men would be good for the East Coast men, too.

The Norfolk and Suffolk coasts were traditionally devoted to fishing, although the number of men involved in the past had been less than in Devon and Cornwall. In the 16th century Devon and Cornwall were estimated to have about 2,000 fishermen each, but Norfolk and Suffolk only about three-quarters of that number. However, the ports of Yarmouth and Lowestoft burgeoned in the 19th century to become the leading fishing centres of the country.

In this they were helped by the investment policy of the Great Eastern Railway, while, sad to relate, the Great Western Railway did little to help fishing in Cornwall.

The East Coast men began to arrive to compete in Cornish waters for mackerel, taken with drift nets. The Brixham men represented less of a threat since they trawled for demersal fish, a practice shunned by Cornish fishermen. Dislike of the 'draggers' who ploughed up the feeding grounds of the fish persisted in Cornwall until recent times. The powerful Brixham trawlers were also somewhat cavalier in their treatment of any drift nets which might lie in their path.

The wider economic results of the coming of fishermen from other coasts may not have been too discernible at the time, but the immediate effect of a necessity of catching the train with fresh fish soon became apparent in a revolution in the design of the Newlyn fishing craft. These vessels were the principal instruments of Newlyn's rise as a fishing port for the rest of the century.

A Mount's Bay lugger making way in a very light breeze. Despite appearances modern experience shows that a Cornish lugger will move in any breeze which will shift a little Mirror sailing dinghy.

In the background is the s.s. *Stormcock* or *Gamecock*. These vessels were chartered in the 1870's by the London & South-Western Railway Company to take Newlyn fish to Plymouth or Southampton, in competition with the Great Western Railway. (*Photo: Vaughan Paul*)

CHAPTER THREE

The Swallows of the Sea

Your luggers – bigger craft. Ah, they – they for example, could often outsail us. They were swallows of the sea.

(A Breton fisherman comparing Cornish boats and Breton crabbers, quoted by L. Luard in *Where the Tides Meet*)

There were three strands in the early evolution of the lug-rigged craft which came to form the Mount's Bay fishing fleet. By the time of the Fisheries Exhibition of 1883 the fleet could be proclaimed by the Committee 'the finest in the world'. The term used for the Mount's Bay boats was not 'drifters' but 'drivers'. Considering that in practice they do drift, as they lie to the train of nets they have shot, the term seems odd. It was borne out of a conflict between two forms of fishing which clashed, not as between men from one region and another, but as between men in the south-west peninsula. The drivers were developed to catch pilchards, not because they were necessarily more efficient in so doing, and therein they came into conflict with the seine fishers. There lay two strands in the story. The third was provided to some degree by the smuggling trade.

The lug rig is an ancient and simple one. The sail can be described as something of a compromise between a square-sail and a fore-and-aft sail. It is set on a yard hoisted up the mast and is loose-footed like a square sail. But the yard is set more of less fore and aft on the mast, according to the point of sailing. It is economical in terms of gear and cordage, while its comparative lightness and the ability to stow the yard on deck and hoist a lighter one by shifting the mizzen sail to the foremast eases the pressure and strain on the vessel. Originally the Cornish lugger carried fore, main and mizzen masts, not unlike the very large versions of the lugger which the French developed. It has been suggested that this press of canvas was developed in response to the need for sail carrying in the smuggling trade, to escape the attentions of revenue cutters.

Because smuggling has been romanticised by the writers of fiction there is naturally a sober tendency to feel that its prevalence and importance have been exaggerated. In cold fact it was big business all around the coast and it has been estimated that during the 18th century it averaged at least thrice the yearly value of pilchards exported. So it may well have been an important influence on design. Certainly when the lugger began to be developed as a fishing vessel the mainmast was dispensed with, for the very simple reason that it took up too much deck space in a boat handling drift nets.

The use of drift nets was a response to economic necessity and a source of conflict with those who used seine nets. Until the 17th century seine-netting had been the established method of catching pilchards. It involved shooting a very large single net to encircle a shoal, close inshore and in shallow water, using a large beamy boat propelled only by oars. The method persisted as a major branch of the industry in Cornwall into this century. As late as 1908 one haul of a seine net brought in £3,000 at Portscatho.

Unlike St. Ives, Newlyn, where inshore conditions were not so favourable, was not destined to develop as a pilchard seining station, but the development of drift net fishing was for economic as well as physical reasons. A seine net was not less than 160 fathoms long and 8 fathoms in depth. It was a single net and hence an indivisible investment. Seining thus became a capitalist enterprise, but in Cornwall the amount of capital available and the number of entrepreneurs willing to invest it was very limited. Mining was always a strong counter attraction. Ultimately the stretches of coast and the number of stations from which seining could be operated were limited.

To the man who could not afford to be a partner in a seine company the answer was drift net fishing involving the setting of a train of nets. Tonkin in his Notes on Carew's 16th century *Survey of Cornwall*, says:-

'Many a poor man, whose purse cannot stretch to part of a seine, may be able to purchase a string of nets and a small boat, by which he may get a very comfortable livelihood for himself and family.'

Tonkin meant, of course, a comfortable livelihood in financial terms. Later on J. S. Courteney in his *Guide to Penzance* of 1845 commented:-

'The drift is the poor man's fishery, the seine that of the capitalist. One provides the boat, one a portion of the nets, a third too poor to produce nets brings nets of a party ashore.'

In later years a normal division of mackerel nets was 15–18 to the skipper, if also the owner; if not 8–10 for the owner and a like number for the skipper, 6–7 nets for the second third and fourth hands. The sixth man and the boy had none and were paid equally. The fleet of nets numbered 42 to 50 and each was a little over 25 fathoms in length. Thus the system of share fishing was something of a co-operative.

In the third strand of the story there is the conflict of the drift net with the established seiners, who believed, or chose to believe, that the drifters interfered with their trade. Either they operated in too close proximity or their activities further out broke up the shoals of pilchards or drove them from the bays. Hence, it is said, the term 'drivers'. As early as 1662 an Act of Parliament limited the activities of the drivers in the summer and autumn months and St. Ives seiners obtained a local Act in 1841. If it is not easy to police fishing in the late 20th century, how much more difficult was it when there was no Fishery Protection Service or Cornwall Sea Fisheries Committee. But actions were nevertheless brought against offenders against the Act until the latter part of the 19th century.

In Mount's Bay there was a remarkable degree of accord between the two factions. The seiners did not think that the drivers were a threat if they kept outside the prescribed limits and would not in any case have impeded the approach of the large shoals. But one and all were united in opposition to the trawlers, which meant the Brixham men. Certainly nothing stood in the way of the development of the Mount's Bay lugger when the impetus for it came.

Back in the latter part of the 18th century the Mount's Bay lugger is described as being only about 25ft in length on the keel, with a raked stem and stern and bluff in the bow. Forward there was a cuddy taking up only 10ft of the length and there the crew slept on the bow sheets. Their cooking caboose was in the open and before the invention of oilskins they had only loose capes of dreadnought cloth as some protection against wet and cold. The open foreroom extended back to the beam thwart with its bulkhead, then came the hold with a gear locker right aft. Sails and spars not in use were stowed on the port side and the net roller was fixed on the starboard side. The full sail plan was formidable and akin to that of the French *Chasse Maree*. The sails were cut squarer but there was jib, foresail, mainsail, main topsail, mizzen, mizzen topsail. In heavy weather the mainmast was unstepped, which could not have been an easy task in a boat with so many spars. It was this class of boat which is said to have gone to Irish waters as early as 1815.

By the 1830's there came a change in design and an increase in size and decking. This was probably a response to the demands of the Irish fishery and also to the provision of a better market with the introduction of the steamer service from Hayle to Bristol. By the middle of the century the size of the luggers had increased to over 40ft and the mainmast was a thing of the past, though confusingly the remaining masts continued to be known as fore and mizzen.

The remarkable sea-keeping qualities of the boats developed in the first half of the century were amply demonstrated by the voyage of the Newlyn lugger *Mystery* at the time of the Crimean War. This vessel had an overall length of 36ft, with a beam of 11ft and 6ft draught and was completely decked for a 12,000 mile voyage to Melbourne for her complement to join the Australian gold rush. It is said that the original idea was to sell the boat to raise the passage money to Melbourne, but as a result of an intemperate evening in a Penzance pub, Captain Richard Nicholls volunteered to skipper her there and next morning refused to lose face by backing out!

Well stored but with only compass, sextant and barometer and the captain's merchant service experience as navigational aids the seven man crew set out nothing daunted, on November 18th 1854. After a week's stay at Cape Town they reached Melbourne on March 14th and delivered Her Majesty's mails with which they had been entrusted at Cape Town. Off Madeira the *Mystery* had spoken an English barque which offered to tell the Australians that they were coming, but the *Mystery* arrived first.

Ocean voyages in small craft are now commonplace, but the idea did not really come into vogue until Captain Slocum's single-handed circumnavigation of the world in the late years of the 19th century. Back in 1928 the *Mystery* would barely have qualified as safe in size for the Fastnet Yacht Race.

The *Mystery*'s feat was therefore outstanding but attracted little notice then (journalism not being what it is now) and little since. The worst weather was experienced running the easting down in the Roaring Forties of the Southern Ocean. The rig of the lugger is not well adapted to heaving-to but at the height of each storm the boat was successfully kept hove-to with a sea-anchor and ran well under bare poles when the weather moderated. Later the ability of the Mount's Bay craft to run successfully in heavy weather was to become an important characteristic.

With the arrival of the railway as far west as Plymouth in 1849 the railway company began to send a cutter to Mount's Bay to load fish. This interest in the fish trade was not entirely matched by the G.W.R. in later years. The local builders set out to produce a hull form to beat the cutter. While there was longer covered accommodation forward, the essential change was in the cross section of the hull, which from being very roughly a U-form became more like a V-form. The first boat to be provided with legs to enable her to take the ground with this shape was the *Volant*, by John Kelynack.

The next step in development was full decking of the boat, with a cabin provided for the crew aft complete with a caboose incorporating an oven for baking.

The ability to put fish on the train at Penzance from 1869 onwards, after the break of gauge at Truro had been overcome, gave the main impetus to design improvements together with the increasing tendency to go ever further into the northern waters of the British Isles and the North Sea. The mackerel drivers increased in size eventually to about 50ft in length, their stems became straight with an only slightly rounded forefoot, and the hull form became progressively sharper in every way. The pilchard drivers evolved in a similar way but remained smaller in size.

The provision of shifting ballast was used to stiffen the boats in their race to catch the train in Penzance, or the steamer in Scilly. The lug retained a disadvantage in that the foresail was a dipping lug so that not only were the crew involved in shifting ballast on going about but the heavy yard had to be dipped around the foremast to go on to the other tack. This required a large crew, but the disadvantage was more apparent than real for the handling of drift nets required a large crew anyway. There were two hands forward, drawing the nets towards the boat and casting off the seizings, two at the capstan, two at the hatch shaking out the fish and stowing the net, and the boy down below in the foot line box, coiling down the warp.

Thus the boats had the crew, power and running ability for quick passages to market before the prevailing winds, and by the same token could extend their range of working.

In the evolution of the design the Newlyn boat had an advantage over St. Ives for a somewhat curious reason. While Newlyn did not have a harbour of serviceable size, St. Ives did. But the harbour at St. Ives was very susceptible to a run of sea in it. Consequently the boats could not stand on legs and had to be rounder in the bilge, with a construction to withstand the 'bumping and boring' which inevitably took place when there was a run of sea. They were also less fine fore and aft than the Mount's Bay boats.

At Newlyn there was only a very small harbour, until late in the century, and the boats mainly stayed on moorings in the 'Loja', off the mouth of the present harbour, which was sheltered from the prevailing winds. In the event of bad weather they went to moorings in the drying part of Penzance harbour, where legs could be used.

It has been suggested that the essentially pointed stern design of the west Cornwall lugger, (there were a few built with counter sterns) was dictated by the necessity of berthing them sardine fashion in the limited harbours. This can hardly be argued in the case of Newlyn, since the medieval harbour was so small that it could only be used by a small portion of the fleet. As in the case of Brixham the number of boats had far outgrown the original facilities of the place. By 1883 Newlyn had 116 mackerel drivers, compared with 60 in 1838. By 1883 there were no seines in Newlyn, but there were 24 pilchard drivers. Mousehole, it may be noted had increased its mackerel drivers from 35 to 60, and in 1893 had 20 pilchard drivers and one seine. During the period the harbour at Mousehole was of a similar size to Newlyn's.

A century ago Newlyn might claim to have a large proportion of the world's finest fishing fleet. It might claim to be a first class fishing station. It could not claim to have a harbour to match, or even much of a harbour at all.

Newlyn in 1882. Work has just commenced on the South Pier. In the foreground is Champion's slip, named after the Headmaster of the Wesleyan School at its head. Opposite is Newlyn slip. The space between the foot of the slip and the road, built in 1908 along the shore, is now occupied by a canning factory. (*Photo: Ben Batten collection*)

Laying the foundation stone of the South Pier at Newlyn by C. C. Ross M.P. on St. Peter's Day, 1884. At the opening ceremony two and a half years later a banner read: 'Welcome to the Newlyn Pier. Long looked for. Come at last. God bless every helping hand'. (*Photo: Reg Watkiss collection*)

CHAPTER FOUR

The Harbour Problem

Newlyn is a poore fisher towne and hath alonly a key for shippes and bootes with lytle socur of land water.
(Leland, 1533)

The old pier at Newlyn is less than 300 ft long and encloses a space which might be described as the half of an oval in shape. It currently provides berths for about two score boats, mainly small craft and punts. Access is by two steep slipways leading down from the Cliff. The one is very narrow and the other leads down from one of the narrowest parts of the road along the Cliff. The construction is of massive granite blocks, without mortar, but the quay is surmounted by a parapet wall in two stages. Part of the parapet was demolished at the end of the last century, but the remainder was saved by the protests of the Newlyn School of artists.

The pier as we see it now is ascribed by one authority to the reign of James the First, but its origin seems to go back into the Middle Ages as there is a record of a pier requiring funds. Although there were some resounding temporal titles attached to Cornwall, such as that of King John's son Richard, who was Earl of Cornwall and King of the Romans, there was a certain lack of local interest on the part of the Lords Temporal. It was left to a Lord Spiritual, Edmund Lacy, Bishop of the Diocese of Exeter, which then included Cornwall, to appeal 'To all who should contribute toward the repairing and maintaining of a certain key or jetty at Newlyn, in the Parish of Paul'. The inducement offered to contributors was forty days indulgence. At the time fishing from Newlyn was not doing too well with hostile French vessels active in the Channel and the appearance of marauders from Spain, not the last occasion on which the Spanish would vex the Parish of Paul.

The first proposal for a new harbour at Newlyn came as early as 1795, but Penzance successfully opposed the Bill in Parliament. This was in the best tradition of competition between ports, who oppose each other's Bills to this day. The enmity between Penzance and Newlyn flourished at least until the two Rugby teams were combined after the Second World War, in a general reaction against violence and bloodshed!

In 1811 Penzance successfully petitioned against another Bill and the idea then seems to have lapsed until the 1860's when it first came up in relation to the idea of a railway between Newlyn and the St. Just mining district. However, a slump in mining in the 1870's killed the idea. A project for a harbour of refuge, which would have been larger than the present harbour, was brought forward about 1870. Newlyn had been formed into a separate parish, out of Paul and Madron, in 1848. The third incumbent, appointed in 1856, was the Rev. John Pope Vibert, son of a Penzance Councillor of the same name. He was an energetic man through whose energy and devotion Newlyn's new church of St. Peter was completed in 1866. He became, no doubt to the annoyance of his father's fellow councillors, Secretary of the harbour project.

Unfortunately the scheme languished for lack of support, even though an Order was obtained and by 1873 the fleet was stated to number 400 boats in the pilchard and mackerel fishery. Nothing altered the fact that if the wind went round to the south'ard and a sea began to build up the Loja became untenable as a roadstead. The only refuge was then in Penzance harbour. Even in fine weather boats which were brought close to the shore took the ground at low water and a night's fishing might be lost waiting for the tide.

Despite all the hazards losses of Newlyn boats were few and certainly rare compared with the North Sea trawlers, but the loss of the 14 ton lugger *Jane* of the highest class, returning from the North Sea fishery on October 7th, 1880, helped to concentrate minds wonderfully. It was the first loss with all hands since May 1840, when the undecked *Dolphin* sank, and had a traumatic effect. Like many another vessel seeking harbour in a gale the *Jane* met disaster in sight of safety. The only refuge was Penzance harbour. About a hundred yards off the entrance a following sea broke over her, but she was held momentarily on the crest before sliding into the trough. Then two seas rebounding off the pier swung the *Jane* right round, rolled her over and she broke in two and sank immediately, with the loss of all seven men on board. It was the first occasion on which a decked lugger had foundered owing to severe weather.

A relief fund was set up by the Mayor of Penzance for the dependants of the crew. One widow, Mrs. Tamsin Williams, continued to draw five shillings (25p) a week from it until her death in 1950. The boat had been insured with the Mount's Bay Fishing Boats' Mutual Insurance Club which had only been registered as a Friendly Society a few months before. The establishment of the club was the result of the efforts of John Pope Vibert's successor as Vicar of Newlyn, the Rev. Wladislaw Somerville Lach-Szyrma. This remarkable man was to go on to play a leading role in organising the building of a new harbour at Newlyn.

If it seems strange that two successive clerics should be so active in this matter we must remember that the founder of the Christian religion gave practical as well as spiritual advice to those fishermen disciples who changed the course of history. 'Cast the net on the right side of the boat and ye shall find': John 21:6. Driftermen traditionally cast their nets on the starboard side and the deck gear is placed accordingly. It was probably a further black mark against the intrusive trawlers that they cast their nets on the port side.

It is more remarkable that community leadership came from the incumbents of the Established Church when the large majority of the inhabitants were chapel-goers, but the Rev. W. J. Burrow, the Wesleyan minister, was on the platform at the first mass meeting at the start of the harbour enterprise and the Rev. T. N. Perkins, another non-conformist was Chairman of the Harbour Commissioners when they were formed. The Anglican leadership is probably explained partly by the fact that the Church of England was more part of the Establishment of the day and its clergymen more in touch with people of influence. In launching any co-operative enterprise the oft-criticised British principle of 'It's not what you know but who you know that matters' is a pragmatically sound one.

But the main reason for the Church of England's lead in this case was that Lach-Szyrma was rather a remarkable man of parts. His father was a Professor at the University of Warsaw who fled to England from his unhappy country after the insurrection of 1830 and married into the Plymouth naval family of Somerville, his bride being Sarah Frances, daughter of Captain Phillip Somerville, R.N., who was with Nelson at Copenhagen. Their son, Wladislaw Somerville, was born on Christmas Day, 1841. Educated at Brasenose College, Oxford he was awarded a classical degree in 1861 and appointed by Bishop Temple to the benefice of Newlyn in 1874. But he had already been a keen student of the fishing industry in Plymouth.

Like many another energetic Anglican clergyman of the period, Lach-Szyrma found time for pursuits outside his pastoral duties. He was a Fellow of the Royal Historical Society, a member of the Archaeological Association and President of the Penzance Natural History and Antiquarian Society just before he left for a parish in Essex in 1891. He wrote *A Short History of Penzance, St. Michael's Mount, St. Ives and the Land's End District*, in which he paid a warm tribute to his predecessor, John Pope Vibert, 'one of the noblest and best of the sons of Penzance'. His little pamphlet on *Newlyn and its Pier*, in 1884, is rather antiquarian in content and does not tell us much of the more recent history of the harbour project.

Lach-Szyrma also wrote a number of religious books, *Pleas for the Faith*, *Thoughts on Clerical Life*, *The Bishopric of Cornwall* and *Short Prayers for the Hours* and, more remarkably, he was a pioneer of science-fiction with *A Voice from Another World* and, in 1884, *Aleric; or a Voyage to Other Worlds*. He gives the impression of having his interests in life very much compartmented.

Lach-Szyrma had been in Newlyn but a few years when there were two losses of fishing boats, the *Primitive* of Mousehole and the *Malakoff* of Newlyn, the latter in collision in 1879. In his words it 'impressed on the boat owners the absolute need of insurance', and a public meeting was organised in the St. Peter's Boys' school, later used as the Newlyn Institute.

A committee was appointed from Newlyn, Mousehole and Porthleven to work out the formation of an insurance club with Lach-Szyrma President. The Club was registered on March 8th, 1880, and by the time of the October storm which sank the *Jane* some 80–100 boats were on the books and the assets are recorded as £80 in the bank. The storm brought claims for £260, including the loss of the *Jane*, but the Mayor of Penzance's Distress Fund produced a residue which replaced the club's loss. The club also pursued the subject of navigation lights for fishing boats and the Board of Trade regulations were amended in accordance with the views of fishermen around the coast.

The loss of the *Jane* and her crew did more than point the value of the Mount's Bay Fishing Boats' Mutual Insurance Club. It made it apparent that a harbour safe to enter would also be a good insurance and provide at the same time all the benefits of berthing, mooring, discharging, and supply facilities. The idea of a large artificial harbour at Newlyn was revived and made into reality with remarkable rapidity, as harbour works go.

The proposal for a harbour at Newlyn involved building a relatively short South Pier and at right angles to it a very long North Pier, leaving an entrance between them facing north-east, subsequently always known as 'The Gaps'. The previous scheme, which had been dropped for lack of support, envisaged a larger 'harbour of refuge'. The harbour of refuge idea had been current in Cornwall for a long time, both for St. Ives Bay and Mount's Bay, the one open to the north and the other open to the south. Indeed the idea of a harbour of refuge on the north coast is still raised from time to time. It had been proposed to build a breakwater across Mount's Bay in the style of the successful one in Plymouth Sound, but sufficient backing was never found and by the end of the century the coming of more powerful steamers and the decline in the number of sailing ships robbed the more grandiose schemes of their impetus.

Nevertheless the second Newlyn scheme embraced no less than forty acres in the most sheltered corner of the bay and would fulfil the function of a harbour of refuge for fishing and coastal craft as well as becoming a fishing port. Apart from the major dock systems of the country, forty acres is no small extent for a harbour. For a comparatively remote part of Britain, 200–300 miles from the main centres of population it could be considered very large.

It would be hard to guess what such a scheme would cost a century on, certainly so many millions that under present legislation Government scrutiny would be very severe. At the time it eventually cost £58,000. Whatever the original estimate may have been the relatively enormous figure for the time must have given pause to even the most self-confident and expansive Victorian mind. In short, where was the money to come from?

The heavy civil engineering cost of building and artificial harbour of any size in the nineteenth century was normally undertaken by a commercial company floated for the purpose, or by a municipality, or one of the great railway companies, or perhaps by major entrepreneurs like the coal barons of South Wales. In Cornwall entrepreneurs built harbours at Charlestown, Par and Newquay, but they were mainly interested in mineral traffic. Minerals indeed were the lure for most entrepreneurial enterprise in Cornwall. Few capitalists were interested in fishing, except the owners of the major seine companies which needed substantial capital backing.

The Great Western Railway became, deservedly, an object of veneration in the West Country, but it showed little interest in encouraging the fish trade. So the Newlyn men were on their own. They were outside the old borough of Penzance and they could expect no help from that quarter, though at least Penzance did not now oppose the scheme.

The only alternative for Newlyn was a co-operative venture. The fishing community was in exactly the same position as a sports club which wishes to build a clubhouse and has no money beyond its members' subscriptions. It must try to raise money by voluntary fund raising efforts and by seeking grants or loans from sympathetic bodies, if possible at a low rate of interest, plus interest-free loans from its own members. In Newlyn that is more or less what the fishermen did. Inevitably the first step was to form a Committee, which took place in 1882. The Chairman was Wladislaw Lach-Szyrma and the Secretary J. Toman. By April 1884 they were ready with plans and draft legislation to go to a mass meeting of the community, held in the Board School, with 350 crammed inside and a 100 standing outside. The man in the chair was Thomas Simon Bolitho, accompanied by Edward Bolitho and Bedford Bolitho. The Bolithos were the major entrepreneurial family of West Cornwall, with interests in banking, mining, tin smelting, ship-owning, seine fishing, the export of pilchards, and in property. Co-operative venture it might be, but the backing of the Bolitho family was a major factor. There can be little doubt that as Chairman of the Fishermen's Committee Lach-Szyrma must have done much to ensure this.

In addressing the meeting Thomas Simon Bolitho made it quite clear that the success of the scheme now rested with the fishermen themselves. A sum of £1,000 would be needed initially for the legislative costs and the purchase of the Old Quay from the Lemon family, who would be paid £500 in cash and £500 in debentures. As in the case of financing the new breakwater at Brixham a levy on fish sold was adopted. In the case of Newlyn it was voluntary and at 2d (1p approx.) in the £. At Brixham the owners of merchant vessels in the port had been poor contributors to the breakwater, but at Newlyn there was no merchant shipping interest of any significance at all which could be called on.

Bolitho went on to say that the main capital would have to come from loans and that the management should be kept in the hands of the fishermen. It was estimated that £35,000 would be needed for the first part of the scheme, including £15,000 for the South Pier. James Inglis, later General Manager of the G.W.R., had been appointed Engineer. There was a certain amount of optimism, as there always is on such occasions, in relation to Government loans and grants. Harbours of refuge were an unfulfilled dream, but the idea was not yet dead and there was a hope of Parliamentary money. Lach-Szyrma wanted a Government grant which would make Newlyn the finest small boat harbour in the country. There were some grounds for optimism as the great International Fisheries Exhibition of the previous year had drawn unusual attention to the industry.

But first the community had to make its own efforts. In the September of 1884 there was a West Cornwall Sea Fisheries Exhibition and a model of the new harbour was put on show. At the same time a bazaar in aid of the scheme was held in Newlyn. In far away Whitby, on the 18th of the month, the Newlyn men there towards the end of the North Sea season put on a concert in aid of funds. By such means and the 2d levy on fish sold the money was there to meet the costs of the Parliamentary Order, which had received Royal Assent by the September.

Bolitho had told the mass meeting that 'a long pull, a strong pull and a pull altogether' would be needed for the scheme, a 'One and all' sentiment often expressed in Cornwall but not always realised. It was calculated that the fish levy would bring in £300 a year and it was to include fish landed to cellars, that is pilchards landed for pressing and subsequent sale. The hope was also expressed that the men of Mousehole and Porthleven would be caught up in the 'One and All' spirit. The Bolithos had made an immediate donation of £100 and Sir John St. Aubyn had contributed £50, but obviously the bulk of the capital would have to come from loans. The various sums involved seem very small to-day but as it is necessary to multiply a 1974 figure by a factor of about four to arrive at a present day price, how much higher must the factor be for an 1884 figure?

The support of the Bolithos was given the lead by Thomas Simon Bolitho who remarked that his father always said that he would rather make a shilling out of fish than half-a-crown out of anything else. On the banking side of the family in 1885 T. Bedford Bolitho offered an advance of £12,000 at 3½% interest and reasonable annual repayments. At the same time there was an interim loan from Batten, Carne and Carne's Bank of Penzance of £15,000. (This local bank crashed in November 1896.)

The first part of the harbour scheme was to be the South Pier, with the lighthouse, which would give a measure of immediate protection from gales from the south. Its 700ft length was constructed with concrete filling and granite facing. A firm foundation was provided by the Carrick-Semmens reef, otherwise known as the Green Rocks. Very little time was lost in preliminaries and St. Peter's Day, June 29th, 1885, was chosen for the laying of the foundation stone by Mr. C. C. Ross, M.P. for the St. Ives division. The community made the most of it and the celebration was declared to be the greatest since the victory at Waterloo. Bunting and other adornments were everywhere, including a model of a rigged boat, evergreen arches and banners with slogans, 'Success to the Pier' and 'God Bless our Harbour of Refuge'. *The Cornishman* newspaper produced an immensely detailed account of the decorations and those who had hung bunting in every street were duly named. By the end of the following year the pier was ready for use, at a reported cost of £20,000.

Work was soon under way on the North Pier, which follows a north-west to south-east line at right angles to the South Pier. The foundation work cannot have been too easy as excavation revealed part of the submerged forest which underlies the inner part of Mount's Bay, or what is properly termed Penzance Bay. (The local name for the Newlyn end is Gwavas Lake.) Nevertheless by 1888 it extended 1,760ft to the Custom House, which is approximately as far as the harbour dries out. It did not reach its present extent until 1894, with a subsequent widening.

July 3rd, 1894 was set as the official opening day, with a memorial stone to be laid by T. Bedford Bolitho, M.P. The *Cornish Telegraph* acclaimed the day with unstinted praise—'Tuesday marked the crown and completion of an enterprise on which the hopes of successive generations of Mount's Bay fishermen have been set, but which only during the last decade has taken tangible shape. Mr. Bolitho, M.P., whose generous help is never solicited more than once in aid of any really deserving cause, has amid every sign of popular rejoicing laid the memorial stone of the magnificent harbour in the western corner of Mount's Bay . . .

'Not many years ago anyone who predicted that the summer of 1894 would witness the performance of such a ceremony would have been laughed at, for during a long period the project of constructing a harbour for Newlyn was placed in much the same category as the proposal to build a breakwater across Mount's Bay.' In other words the community had rather surprised itself at its own success. Bedford Bolitho admitted that ten years before it would not have been thought possible to borrow the £53,000 necessary.

Lach-Szyrma was unfortunately unable to be present on that fine July day in 1894 and sent his apologies for absence. His successor, the Rev. T. Norwood Perkins had become Chairman of the Harbour Commissioners. Principal speeches were made by Major Ross, deputising for the local M.P., Mr. C. C. Ross, and by the Mayor of Penzance. The Major had an accurate view of the future, looking forward to stately warehouses on the Cliff and hills and terraces crowned with the villas of merchant princes; if one allows that there are not too many merchant princes in modern Newlyn. He did not think Penzance would suffer and, again accurately, foresaw that Penzance and Newlyn would become one big town. This came to pass with the extension of the borough of Penzance in 1934 and the growing together of the two built-areas, which is not to say that their respective identities were submerged.

The Mayor of Penzance, William Harvey Julyan, agreed that there was room for both communities and said that he had come mainly to hold out 'the right hand of fellowship'. This phrase, derived from Galatians Ch. 9 v.2, seems to have been a popular sentiment with the Victorians, as it appears again in Newlyn's story in a less happy context. Moreover in the next two years it was proved that Penzance would be quick to snatch away its right hand of fellowship. For the time being all was harmony and the festivities of the day again included the evergreen arches, displays of bunting and the banners inscribed 'Success to our Harbour'. The population of Newlyn at the time was approaching 4,000 and no less that 1,600 school children were assembled for the celebration to emphasise the importance of the new harbour to future generations.

The most significant comment of the day was made by Bedford Bolitho himself, who said that the harbour would be of benefit to fishermen from all parts of the country. Such expansive and optimistic remarks on celebratory occasions often fall into the category of mere rhetoric. But this prediction proved to be all too shrewd for the men of Newlyn. Within two years the use of the new harbour by fishermen from other parts of the country was to lead to the riots of May 1896 and a bitter quarrel with the town of Penzance.

Newlyn is an international harbour of refuge. A winter gale in 1987 accounts for the tiers of Belgian trawlers to the fore. (*Photo: John Corin*)

An idealised Frith portrait of Newlyn people. The woman is carrying a fish-wife's cowl, used for hawking fish and carrying them from the boats to the pil-chard cellars. These baskets contained 300 pilchards, or three-quarters of a hundredweight approximately. (*Photo: Frith*)

CHAPTER FIVE

Work And Home

Toil on, toil on,
And in thy toil rejoice
(Old Methodist hymn)

Newlyn, with yet another pier added within the harbour in recent years, has become the fourth fishing port in the British Isles in terms of value of fish landed. That this should be so is a tribute to the endeavours of Newlyn people a century ago, under the leadership of Lach-Szyrma, the Bolithos and their colleagues.

When the new harbour, encompassing 40 acres, was first completed and available for use it could hardly fail to be an instant operational success. The small medieval harbour, which might at best contain 40 boats squeezed together, was a thing of the past. The necessity to abandon the moorings in the Loja in the face of heavy weather from the south and run for the drying part of Penzance harbour was no more. Indeed the Loja was no more as far as local boats were concerned. There was now 'The Gaps', the entrance between the North and South Piers, which it is claimed has never been closed. Indeed Newlyn became a harbour of refuge and much more effective as such than Penzance, it being possible to enter not only with any weather but at any state of the tide.

The great operational advance was reflected in the financial results. In 1888 the total of dues taken was £1,387. In 1894, the year of the opening of the North Pier, dues revenue increased by nearly 50% to £2,054, and not all of the new revenue came from Newlyn boats. Bedford Bolitho's prophecy began to come true almost immediately. What was good for the Newlyn men was good for the East Coast men, who had come for the mackerel season for many years, for the powerful trawlers of Brixham and for Breton crabbers.

Writing to *The Cornishman* newspaper some half a century later, Francis de Rouffignac of Newlyn recalled that the plans for the new harbour, with their ambitious scale, had not met with the approval of 'One and All' in Newlyn. 'The older men wanted a harbour, certainly, but they did not want it to be either as big, or as well equipped, as did the young men. 'You build a great harbour', they told their sons and nephews, 'and strangers will come and fish with bigger boats and better gear than you have; on the nights when you are in the harbour they will poach, and you will be starved out.' In the short term the old men's judgement was shrewd. Although in the long term the younger men were proved correct their optimism gave way in 1896 to the bitter conflict which ensued with the East Coast men.

To understand what caused the flare-up of the Newlyn Riots it is necessary to understand the kind of community which Newlyn people formed, and the differences between it and the community to which the East Coast men belonged. A large proportion of the people living in Newlyn today were not born in Cornwall and have no family links, so can gain little idea of life in Newlyn a century ago and nor can those locals whose memories do not go back as far as the 1930s. For in the 1930s the Victorian way of life lingered on. It has been said, with some justice, that in the provinces the Victorian era did not end until the Second World War. Only older people will have some picture in their minds of life in Newlyn in the 1890's, but fortunately some published and unpublished records survive. Wilkie Collins and W. H. Hudson, for instance, have left brilliant vignettes of some aspects, while the writer of Cornish stories, Charles Lee, shows Newlyn in the rather antiseptic style of treatment of some Victorian writers. However his inclusion of certain recognisable personalities was sufficiently accurate to make him unpopular in Newlyn.

In the early 1930's Miss Janie Kelynack prepared two papers for the Camborne Old Cornwall Society. They described her memories of Newlyn, which went back well into the previous century. Her precise descriptions of domestic life and reflections on the fishing industry, which that life was intimately associated, are of the greatest value. Recently Mrs. Blanche Brown has written some memoirs of life in the village in the early part of this century, when not a great deal had changed and these are equally valuable. To these may be added the publications of Ben Batten who has recorded so much of Newlyn's history and topography.

The character of the houses in Newlyn in the 19th century is a sound guide to the economic and social condition of the people. (It would not be so simple a guide in this century.) The study of Newlyn's houses has been simplified by the Spanish raid of 1595, when the village, along with Paul, Mousehole and Penzance, was burnt, so that unfortunately there is nothing left of significance before that date. Further destruction was wrought by the insensitivity of the borough of Penzance in its housing policy in the 1930's. Fortunately sufficient remains to distinguish two main types of dwellings, which may be broadly described as 'courtyard' and 'terrace'. The latter are simply defined. A building boom seems to have started in the 1880s and led to the construction of fairly standard four-square small houses, mainly in groups or terraces. Some were built on new sites, as on and behind New Road, at the eastern end of the village. Others were inserted in the old parts of the village. Later two terraces of more imposing Victorian villas were built further up the hillside. In character they resembled those built in Alexandra Road and Morrab Road in Penzance, where the former had been built much earlier, in 1865. A section of Newlyn's population was obviously catching up in prosperity: but the smaller terrace houses in Newlyn were more typical. They were built of granite, sometimes with a mixture of other local stone, killas and elvan, while others were of fine cut granite. In any case their function was usually purely domestic, in contrast to the older courtyard type houses.

The courtyard buildings would justify defining the pilchard fishery as literally a 'cottage industry'. They moulded together the domestic and industrial life of the people in inescapable union. They are not easily described, although recognisable examples survive in domesticated form in Newlyn and Mousehole. Essentially the lower storey was entered by a door wide enough to admit a fish barrel. The centre of the court was open to the sky and might contain a peeth (well) which supplied cold water for fish washing and domestic purposes. Around the side were the cellars, dark and cool, in which cured fish were stored and also fishermen's gear. The dwellings were in fact flats above, with two or three rooms, perhaps approached by exterior steps. There were variations on this theme where a court might be partly lined with linhays, or lean-to's. There were also more detached buildings, with flat above and cellar beneath. Examples of the latter may be most easily detected in Mousehole. Jumbled in amongst this kind of development were the co-operative salting cellars for pilchards which were also quadrangles open to the sky in the centre and roofed in along the sides or with dwellings above. There are still discernible in Newlyn walls with a row of rectangular holes a few feet from the ground. These holes held the ends of the pressing bars which bore down on the heads of the hogsheads of pilchards. They were weighted on the other end by egg shaped granite 'pressing stones'. Examples may be seen near the Red Lion in Newlyn of both the old cellar walls and the pressing stones.

W. H. Hudson, the naturalist, described St. Ives eighty years ago and his description would have equally well fitted Newlyn at the time: 'The houses are closely packed, or rather jumbled together with the narrowest and crookedest street and courts in which to get about or up and down. They have a look of individuality, like a crowd of big rough men pushing and elbowing one another for room.'

Wilkie Collins in his *Rambles Beyond Railways*, first published in 1851, gives a vivid and accurate description of the scene in the fish cellars when a catch was *bulked* for pressing into hogsheads and eventual export. Janie Kelynack has left a shorter but very clear account of the process in the cellars:-

> Eager hands await the harvest of the sea and the precious burden is carried by men, women and children up the slipways and stiff streets to the cellars in readiness to receive them.
>
> Horses and carts toil up the inclines by the aid of torches as the night advances. Women bend under the weight of their cowals. One might see three persons carrying two baskets of fish between them and children following picking what fell out of the baskets.
>
> Now let us look at the cellar. It is a big stone-paved court with lofts, or the dwelling house, over parts, these being supported by tall granite pillars. The covered portion is paved closely with very small oval stones in cambered strips, divisions being made for drainage with long narrow pieces of wood. The other portion is open to the sky. About four or five feet above the pavement and at intervals along the walls are square apertures to accommodate the ends of the long beams, or pressing poles.
>
> When the pilchards reached their destination the whole cellar

> was illumined by candles, and everyone was busy till far into the night. As soon as daylight appeared men and women were again in the cellars to start the curing of the fish.
>
> *Bulking* was the first process. This meant the forming of huge piles of pilchards on the small paving stones, in alternate layers of fish and salt, the outer row showing all the fishes' heads. These *bulks* were allowed to remain three weeks before the fish were considered cured and fit to *break out*.
>
> Now the salted pilchards, known as *fairmaids*, were washed in a *kieve*, or huge wooden tray having a grating in the bottom through which the fish scales could drop. From this the pilchards were lifted on a big griddle into a wooden stand, having a barred bottom, on high legs. This stand containing the fish was carried by two men to the women already waiting to pack the *fairmaids* into hogsheads, numbers of which were standing in readiness against the walls, under the apertures.
>
> Each woman placed as many fish as she could on her open palm in the shape of a fan and placed them in the hogshead, head to cask, until the circle was complete. The centre, called the *rose*, was filled in alternately head and tail, this being repeated until the cask was full. A heavy wooden cover, called a *buckler* was next placed on top, with blocks on its inner side for leverage.
>
> A long pressing pole inserted in the aperture above and projecting some distance beyond the cask, was weighted at the end by means of a big rounded pressing stone hung by a rope, and so the fish were pressed for two or three hours. At the end of this time the cask needed a refill. Twenty four hours later a further repacking was necessary and at the end of two days the final *back-laying* was done. This time all the backs of the fish were uppermost. Two thousand *fairmaids* were now in each hogshead and the whole had a last pressing before the cooper came to *head in* the cask.

Collins records that the women and girls were paid at the rate of threepence (1p) an hour plus a glass of brandy and a piece of bread and cheese every sixth hour. For various reasons brandy was not relatively so expensive in Cornwall at that time. He also mentions a local side benefit in the accepted practice of *kybing* pilchards. As the barrows went through the gateways into the salting cellars local boys endeavoured to snatch fish off the pile, a contest which was made sporting by the employment of a boy with a cane who endeavoured with varying success to smite their hands.

From the bulking and pressing process nothing was wasted. The oil exuded from the fish was sold for refining. The *drugs*, or scum, were sold for lubricating oil and the discarded salt for fertiliser. The filled hogsheads of fairmaids, were examined and approved by the buyers' agents and taken for export. At one time the fast fruit schooners on the Mediterranean run took the pilchards as an outward cargo, but they were succeeded by steamers which berthed on the North Pier.

'Fairmaid' was a happy Cornish corruption of the Spanish *fumados*, a term originally applied to smoked fish. The demand for fish in Roman Catholic countries in southern Europe made the Pope a popular man among the Non-Conformist fishermen of Cornwall and gave rise to the well known toast:

Long life to the Pope:
Death to our best friends:
And may our streets run in blood:

The friends were the pilchards and the blood that which exuded in the cellars.

Such an intimate relationship between pilchard processing and housing would horrify a modern environmental health officer and the smell of fish must have permeated everywhere. Perhaps like those accustomed to the smell of silage on a farm the inhabitants never noticed it. The visitors did. Murray's *Handbook for Travellers in Devon & Cornwall, 1850*, remarked on 'Those antiquated fishing towns which are viewed more agreeably from a distance' – not the stuff of modern tourist brochures.

If the streets, alleyways and courts were smelly and irregular, inside the houses there was good, even stereotyped order. Janie Kelynack takes us to a modest fisherman's cottage and says:

> We will look into the living room, which is large and comfortable.
>
> In front of the window, draped with a meshed and darned curtain, stands a big table for meals. In a corner is a small round table with lower shelf.
>
> Against the wall opposite the window is a mahogany 'back'

table on which reposes the Family Bible. A pile of books on either side rises in graduated sizes, and a case of pretty stuffed birds, or a vase of artificial flowers made of shells, and protected by a glass shade, occupies the central position. Forming a background is a set of three 'waiters' arranged one behind the other. The leaf of the table is turned down to show the high polish, and under the end of this is tucked the duster.

The corner by the fireplace is occupied by a buffet with glass door, through which one sees the best china, glass ware and silver teaspoons, the latter arranged in threes, fanwise with bowls uppermost.

A copper warming pan, so highly polished, hangs on one side of the shining fire-range. This treasure is the pride of the housewife being, 'like Evangeline's ear-rings, handed down from mother to child through long generations.'

On the opposite side of the fireplace hangs the 'billes' (bellows) underneath which stands a four-legged green stool, used to sit on when the fire needs the bellows.

On the mantel shelf are arranged china dogs or other figures and brass candlesticks. Behind these hang a pair of glass rollers brought from some distant port, Whitby or Scarborough.

At right angles to the fireplace is a high-backed settle and, for the comfort of those who sit around the fireside, a long manilla mat lies on the floor. The mat is home made.

At the foot of the staircase which leads to the bedrooms above, a 'reel' to hold hanks of cotton for net-making is attached to the newel post.

A few green chairs with barred backs complete the furniture.

In his *Harbour Village*, describing his childhood in Mousehole, Leo Tregenza gives a sensitive description of his memory of entering just such a room as a child:

I passed in under the cloisters below the loft, came to the open door of the little cottage and walked into the main room. There was a small window by the far corner that seemed to look out on to someone else's yard, a table with a couple of chairs in the middle, an open dresser on the left and darker side away from the window, and an armchair and a fire in the grate on the right. On the mantelpiece there was a clock, one or two ornaments I can't now visualise, a pair of steel-rimmed reading spectacles, a woman's purse, old and worn, and a few coppers by its side. Above the clock was a framed photograph of an old man, obviously the father, or grandfather of the wife or her husband.

I don't know to what extent I sensed the atmosphere of this living room when I entered it then as a child, but I became familiar with its like as the years went by, and remembering it now realise that all the typical ingredients were there; the sound of the clock accentuating the silence of the small room; a bible no doubt, a necessary part of the furniture; the quiet fire; and that purse with the loose coins near it: a picture eloquent of a way of life in which the material wealth of this world played no great part, of a life of honest toil, of the sadness perhaps as well as the joys that were a part of it. And that photograph of the old bearded fisherman in his suit of dark serge, sitting up straight and rather stiffly in his chair, his hands resting on the arms, how typical too. The older these portraits are the more clearly they seem to speak of the past. The story of their lives is written on their faces as if it has been inscribed in a village Book of Days.

Within these quiet houses the facilities for living were minimal. Heating and cooking was provided for by open fires and perhaps a cooking range or slab. Refrigeration was based on a cold pantry or a little outside cupboard with a gauze door. For lighting paraffin lamps had superseded the use of pilchard oil. (The pilchard catch used to be said to provide 'meat, money and light, all in one night'.) The glow from the windows of the houses served for street lighting, supplementing the heavenly body termed 'the parish lantern'.

There was no inside water supply, which had to be obtained from wells or a small number of 'shoats' or water shoots.

If life ashore was spartan, it was even more so afloat, especially when the boats were away on distant fishing grounds around the British Isles. One amenity which the majority of houses lacked in the crowded streets was any sort of outlook or the sea-views beloved of modern house agents. Indeed many houses in Newlyn were, and are, subject to poor natural lighting through the windows. Of one thing we may be sure, the fishermen did not particularly desire a sea-view when they were at home!

The lack of facilities inside the houses promoted community life to no small extent. People met at the shoats to collect water and the women also met in the bakehouses which provided a service for those with inadequate cooking arrangements at home, not to mention a 'dry' over the oven where many a customer's wet suit was hung in winter. There were at one time five such bakehouses in Newlyn and the last was Angwin's, next to the Red Lion. To these establishments the housewives brought their loaves to be baked each day, also dinners, cakes and other items like marinated pilchards, which were baked overnight. One may be sure that while all were gathered together silence did not prevail. At one bakehouse proceedings were enlivened, according to Janie Kelynack, by a colt which was in the habit of escaping from its stable and invading the place.

Doorstep delivery of milk was unknown and it had to be fetched from Gwavas Farm or a farm on Paul Hill or even as far away as Tredavoe. On market day in Penzance housewives trudged there to shop, armed with a deep basket to bring home groceries to last for a week.

Life at home was occupied fully with work throughout the week and an immutable routine was followed. On wash day much water had to be fetched in buckets or pitchers, but heavy items such as counterpanes, mats and men's sea clothes were first streamed under one of the shoats. At home clothes were boiled in a copper vessel. In winter they were dried in the linhays of the courtyard houses and in summer on bushes in various fields. The Cornish furze bush makes a good clothes line. Mangling was done by a communal box mangle of ponderous construction. What with fetching the water, taking the clothes out to dry and meeting for the mangling service there was plenty of opportunity for everybody to meet everybody else and exchange information. So that apart from the innumerable ties of relationship in an inter-marrying community everyone had a good knowledge of everyone else's business. A measure of this intimacy was the proliferation of nick-names, which remained in use for a lifetime, perhaps long after the original reason for the name had been generally forgotten.

Apart from breaks for a little bit of chat, domestic work followed an inexorable weekly round of cooking, shopping and housework. Thursday was 'bedroom day' and Friday was 'kitchen day', the latter involving a major exercise of cleaning 'the slab' and all the brasses, including perhaps a host of brass stair rods.

Time also had to be set aside for mending clothes, particularly the men's heavy sea-going clothes. Guernseys were knitted at home on eight stocking needles using four-ply wool. Sea-boot stockings, three-quarters length stockings, children's clothes were all knitted at home and there was always plenty of sewing. Daughters of the house found a winter evening occupation in 'breeding' (making) nets seated around the dining table, plying wooden needles. One of the smaller children filled the needles or twisted the 'ossels' (norsils) for attaching the nets to the ropes.

Apart from the employment of women in the cellars in the pilchard season, there were others who made a living selling fish retail. These women walked for many miles, bearing a heavy burden of fish and salt. The former was carried in a 'cawal', a big basket shaped for easy carriage on the back, and held in place by a broad band across the forehead. The chafe was taken by a poke bonnet which had a white goffered frill framing the face. The woman's back was protected by the 'turnover', a woollen shawl folded corner-wise, the ends crossed in front, and these with the point at the back, caught down securely to a snow white apron worn over a full skirt.

If the women of the village were kept fully employed industrially or domestically, feminists should not imagine that the men were what women call 'helpless' in domestic matters. Like all good sailors they were quite capable of looking after themselves. For their spells on the distant water fishing grounds they had to be. For an absence of several months they victualled their boat with salt beef, butter, dried onions, sacks of caraway seeds, and ships' biscuits the size of tea plates from Beckerleg's in Bread Street, Penzance. It was said that the fleet could be followed to Ireland by a trail of cabbage leaves.

In their time away the men had to look after their own clothes and be self-sufficient, living in a crowded and cramped cabin, with few of what a modern sailor would consider to be basic amenities. They did not fail to bring gifts home from distant parts, Paisley shawls, or shawls from the Shetlands, sheep skin rugs, jet alberts and brooches from Whitby.

The interior of a typical West Penwith cottage c. 1880. Any kitchen/living room in Newlyn would have been basically very similar. The kitchen range, or 'slab', in the left hand corner would have been made in a local foundry. (*Photo: Reg Watkiss collection*)

A Newlyn fishwife filling in a little time by knitting. The site is that of the later fish market. In the background, right, is the sign of J. Uren, Sailmaker. The sign board behind the woman is that of Clemens & Davies. The bottom line reads 'Fitters etc.', but the middle line is indecipherable. In the distance is the Newlyn Ice Store of R. R. Bath and the office of B. J. Ridge, fish salesman, where the Ice Works now stands. (*Photo: Alfred Robinson*)

CHAPTER SIX

A Clash of Cultures

It is a pity that those who wrote and talked so freely about the Riots, both in and out of Parliament, could not have had a better understanding of the real motives and political economy of this Cornish protest against East Anglian greed.

(F. G. Aflalo in *The Sea-Fishing Industry*, 1904)

The work load for Newlyn people was not quite endless. The Sabbath was kept holy. In the case of the Primitive Methodists the young children were only allowed out of the house on Sundays to go to Sunday School. Older children graduated to going to chapel in the morning, Sunday School in the afternoon and chapel in the evening. When they were older still this strict routine was relieved by being allowed to go to Penzance Promenade on Sunday evenings, until 9 pm in the winter and 9.30 pm in the summer.

Newlyn, like most Cornish fishing and mining villages was strongly non-conformist. Until the coming of John Wesley the industrial population of Cornwall was sorely neglected by the Established church. To Milton, 'The hungry sheep looked up and were not fed'. Wesley initially met violent resistance from poverty stricken and godless men, but once his persistence had converted them Celtic fervour took over and the pendulum swung the other way. This process was greatly enhanced by the passion for singing which extended into and out of the chapels, helped by the Methodist Hymn Book and such local talent as that of Thomas Merritt of Illogan, whose carols so outshine those of Hymns A. & M.

An educational effect of the Methodist church on the adult population came through its system of government. Congregations had the task of running their own chapel affairs within the circuit and also of providing lay preachers. By contrast the Church of England was not formally democratised at parish level until an Act of 1919.

Before the 1870 Education Act secular education was confined to some dame schools, with a few girls being sent to schools in Penzance. The first National School was at Paul, with the parish clerk as schoolmaster. He was succeeded by James Richards, who taught navigation as an extra-curricular subject. Adult education was limited to 'penny readings' and in the afternoons many women brought their knitting to the cooper's house in Cooper's Court for readings of *Uncle Tom's Cabin, Hiawatha* and other best-sellers of the day.

Formal group leisure activities were not well catered for, except for periodical junketings and galas connected with church and chapel, and older pagan events like the Midsummer Eve bonfires, with blazing tar-barrels and torches. Conversation was probably still the chief leisure activity. We have seen the various places in which the women gathered. The men were accustomed to meet and talk on the Cliff. Traditionally this was formalised into a number of groups, or 'gows', where a man did not stray to another group unless invited. Indoor conversation, on a men only basis, was conducted by a group gathered on long seats in the cobbler's shop, a scene which appears in Charles Lee's *Our Little Town*.

If the condition of souls in the community was very well catered for, and the health of the mind reasonably encouraged, then the care of the body was not very well served. Indeed the cobbler, besides providing a social centre, acted as dentist, to the extent of drawing teeth. There was no doctor's surgery in Newlyn and nor is there one to-day. Later St. Peter's Club provided a club doctor, but he generally had to be sent for from Penzance. For minor medical matters there seems to have been an informal arrangement whereby some fishermen's wives acted as district nurses. They also functioned as midwives in the days before formal training was considered necessary.

Public services, as we know them today, were thus obviously not very well-developed in Newlyn. The police presence was limited to one constable of the county force, for approximately 4,000 people. There is no evidence that in normal times this was not adequate cover. Newlyn, under the influence of Methodism and the associated temperance, was on the whole well-behaved. Penzance, with its borough police force and about three times the population had about one policeman per thousand of the population, but being a market town and port for commercial shipping was less well-behaved. There was an area of poor housing in the streets leading down to the harbour and violence in Penzance a hundred years ago, or even fifty years ago, was more common than is generally realised. There were also a very large number of pubs in Penzance. There still are, not only prominent ones, but in unlikely side streets and odd corners of the town. Even today Penzance is distinguished by having twice the national average of off-licences per head of population. By contrast there have never been more than about half a dozen pubs in Newlyn.

The Newlyn community was largely self-regulating. Charles Lee in his tale *The Widow Woman*, in which Newlyn appears all too thinly disguised as 'Pendennack', puts his finger on it: 'Small wonder that crime should be rare in Pendennack, where the art of divination by straws has attained such rare perfection. The secret plotter may lock himself in a back chamber and draw the blinds, but, with Pendennack women-folk about, he might as well go bawl his plans from the pier-head at once. Stone walls and locked doors avail nothing against their penetration.'

Obviously the daily lives and routines of everyone living in close-packed housing were always well-known to neighbours and the innumerable relations everybody acquired since most marriages were within the village. Any unusual, let alone criminal, activity would be speedily noted.

This is illustrated by a tale from a fishing village not a hundred miles from Newlyn. The story also shows that a wrong-doer could be subtly brought to justice without the intervention of the Law, or even anything being said.

A certain woman knew for a fact that a neighbour had stolen a chicken. Whether the theft could be actually proved or not was irrelevant. It would obviously be too damaging and dangerous to make any open accusation, still more so to report the matter. What to do? The miscreant knew that her theft was known to her neighbour and her neighbour knew that she knew so! The latter's solution was an elegant one. Being sure that the thief would roast the chicken in the oven for the next Sunday dinner, sometime before the hour she called on her on some pretext and detained her in conversation so long that she had the choice of removing the object of her guilt from the oven or letting it spoil beyond redemption. She chose the latter course and her silent accuser retired well satisfied.

How did the people of Newlyn, who led such a blameless community life, with little need for formal policing, come to erupt into the violence of May 1896 which led the authorities to despatch naval vessels and hundreds of armed troops to Mount's Bay? The answer must lie in a study of the differences between the two communities involved in this 'communal riot'. This embraces not only their obvious religious and economic differences, which were well publicised, but in the organisation of their industry and their approach to life.

In the course of the riots of May 1896 the Newlyn Fishermen's Committee issued a statement outlining their views on Sunday fishing and attitude of the East Coast men. In the first sentence they said that they believed 'that if the Sabbath is kept it will be better for us not only in the religious but in the pecuniary sense'. This blend of candour and hypocrisy may bring a sneer to the lips of an Englishman and a smile to the face of any true Cornishmen. Cornishmen may be proud of being devout but they also like to feel that they are hard men when it comes to pecuniary advantage. At the same time they may contrive to persuade the stranger that they are guileless.

However, their basic difficulty in Newlyn was that they could not object to East Coast, or any other men, fishing in what might be deemed to be Cornish waters. This for the simple reason that in the course of a year they themselves fished all around the British Isles and made ports far away their temporary base.

However, the East Coast drifters were substantially larger and faster. A typical Mount's Bay mackerel driver was 50–52 ft long, while a typical East Coast drifter was 64 ft long, with a gaff rig giving a much larger sail area when tops'ls and heads'ls were set. There was a larger crew of nine or more. These company-owned vessels thus had to earn a greater return, which they did with longer trains of nets.

Did the Newlyn men feel economic hardship from the competition? How well, or badly off, was the community? Even today with a mass of statistics available in relation to incomes and prices it is hard to arrive at a true reading of the economic state of any particular area. This is because the symptoms of income and expenditure can seldom be directly related locally to national and regional averages or the percentage of the population shown by the statistics to be living in poverty. In other words the numbers of new cars, the number of people in the pubs or the expenditure on children's Christmas presents may seem to belie the statistics. Effects must always be uneven. Even in the hard times of the 1930's there were remarkable anomalies.

Figures for earnings in Newlyn at the time of the riots are hard to come by, if for no other reason than that under the share system they fluctuated widely. The average earnings of Mount's Bay men are said to have declined from £40 a year to £15 or less. These figures can be compared with an advertisement at the time for an Inspector of Nuisances issued by the Port Sanitary Authority Joint Board which offered a salary of £20 per annum. A member of the Fishermen's Committee averred that 'where I ought to get £5 for my share of the week's work I have had to take four or five shillings (20 or 25p). The Lowestoft men got 16s (80p) a 100 for their Sunday fish, and we only get five shillings (25p) for what we brought in on the Tuesday. Then the other day I landed 7,500 mackerel, which realised £12.13s (£12.65), out of which expenses and commission absorbed three shillings (15p) in the £1. That left for each of the men only 7 or 8s a share (35 or 40p).'

It must be remembered that the Newlyn men were only in competition locally with the East Coast men for the mackerel season part of the year. Nevertheless earnings would have been irregular at all times of the year and the housewife would always have to manage the domestic budget very carefully. Every economy was adopted in relation to food and the provision of clothing, the latter by knitting and home sewing and the former by careful storage and preservation. In the autumn when income was fairly good, and prices lower, sacks of flour, winter onions, salt butter and late potatoes were laid by. Hake, cod and ling were salted in large trays and dried on walls until hard as a board. This fish was ultimately eaten as the famous 'tow-rag'. Pilchards were, of course, salted down in large quantities in 'bussas', large earthenware jars. Even eggs were bought up when cheap and pickled for use in cooking in the winter.

The dead of winter, between any of the fishing seasons, when a succession of gales could keep the men ashore anyway, was the most difficult time of year for the household budget. Then traders gave credit until the spring and in very needy cases the local gentry gave relief through the medium of trusted fish salesmen. Nevertheless the pawnbroker was unknown in Newlyn and there was only one in Penzance. There was no social security and not much in the way of alternative employment near at hand. Enlistment in the naval reserve was the only help the State offered, and that was minimal. On occasions the men sought temporary employment as surface workers at the St. Just mines. On Sunday evenings they walked the six miles there to be in time for the Monday morning shift. With them they took their white 'dowlas' seabag with provisions to reduce the board and lodging charges. There survives a very large house in the hamlet of Kenidjack which is believed to have been a lodging house.

The miners probably suffered more than the fishermen from periodical hard times and generally speaking were worse off. Miners' wages have been put at an average of 18s (90p) to £1 per week or even as low as £2 or £2.10s (£2.50) a month. Tributers who worked on a piece work basis might earn as much as £6.10s per month (£6.50). Estimates vary between mines and districts. Even if fishermen's averages were sometimes equally low their families were better fed, if only for the simple reason that some fish were very cheap and there were probably few families who did not receive some free fish from a catch.

Houses in Newlyn were much more sheltered than the poor rows of miners' cottages in the St. Just district, and after about 1880 much more substantially built. Above all the fishermen led healthier, safer lives, compared with the miners who might walk miles to work, climb down a hundred fathoms or two of ladders and ascend at the end of a shift, carrying their tools, to emerge from a hot mine into winter weather with clothing already wet. Safety conditions underground were at a very low standard. Nevertheless, writing in 1883 in *The Economic Condition of Fishermen* Professor Leone Lewis asked 'Is the remuneration of fishermen for so much fatigue adequate? Alas, No.' and W. M. Adams said in the same year: 'There is no trade or occupation so peculiarly distinguished through all times and all nations by the poverty of its pursuers as that of fishing.' So how poor were the fishing people of Newlyn at this time? The answer from all the evidence of their way of life must be that while few were affluent by the standard of the day – piano in the front room – and many could not afford a cooking range or mangle, few lived in poverty. Large families would have been a problem, but relations were very supportive and family ties very close knit, especially in the care of children and old people.

What is certain is that they managed to survive without fishing on

Sundays, despite the competition in the mackerel season. It has even been suggested that they did not always set out to earn as much as they might have done. Charles Lee in his Newlyn tale *The Widow Woman* gives voice to this suspicion in the following passage: 'When the information reached Uncle Billy, he called 'Nezer Harvey and Dickon Tremethick into consultation, and it was quickly decided that the weather, in spite of clear sky and steady breeze, was decidedly "foxy", and that it would be the height of imprudence to venture out short-handed. This decision is so regular on such occasions, and savours so much of the formula, that it might be held to give colour to the slanderous statement of a certain foreigner, who said that the week in Pendennack is divided into three portions – days when the men mustn't go out (Saturday and Sunday), days when they can't, and days when they won't.' The relaying of this statement doubtless did little to increase Lee's local popularity, where he had already given offence by too recognisable characterisation of certain individuals.

There will always be fishermen more willing to go to sea in doubtful conditions than others and it can be argued that the Cornish, as a group, merely behaved as the 'prudent mariner' beloved of the manuals of seamanship then, and of the rescue services today. Certainly the accident record for Newlyn boats compares very favourably indeed with that of the East Coast, by any criterion. In the case of Hull even the existence of a much larger fleet can hardly excuse losses such as December 1863, 24 smacks and 144 lives, March 1877, 36 smacks and 215 lives, December 1894, 106 men in a single day. Between 1878 and 1882 the death rate for Hull's fishermen reached 1% in casualties at sea. There are no figures available for Newlyn which can be directly compared, but as noted already losses of fishing vessels from Mount's Bay in this period were comparatively rare. This is emphasised by the great impact which the loss of the *Jane* in 1880 had on the community. It was an exceptional event.

Part of the answer for this discrepancy is that the East Coast men worked as employees for the owners of their vessels under a system in which while they were dependent on the results of their work they were obliged to work as the owners directed. For example, when steamers were first employed to collect catches from trawlers in the North Sea instead of the trawler having to return to harbour with a catch (the notorious 'fleeting' system) the wretched fishermen were kept at sea for up to two months. Under their share system the Cornish had a much more relaxed approach to their work and as the complicated division of nets shows it was a co-operative approach. One of the comments made by the Lowestoft men at the time of the riots was that they would be happy not to fish on Sundays, if only the owners would allow it.

The division of the share money among the Newlyn crew at the end of the week was distinctly informal. The men called at the house of the owner/skipper or of the family owning the boat and collected their money off the kitchen mantelpiece. Charles Lee's widow woman, in his tale of that name, was exceptional in that the crew all collected their money at the same time from her house and there was a conference at which the boat's business and operational problems were sorted out with advantage in everyone's presence. Lee comments that such a determined plan was 'foreign to Pendennack's dilatory, haphazard business methods'. Strangers still complain about a dilatory approach to business by Cornishmen, and also complain about the ulcers they themselves have developed as a result of more high pressure methods.

The Cornish proclivity to share fishing is demonstrated by a recent story in Newlyn. A new seiner, *Dew-Genen-Ny*, appeared in harbour. Two old skippers were on the quay. '*Dew-genen-ny*! Wass that mean then Joe?'. 'Why es Cornish for God is with us'. 'Aw, well thass another share gone then!'

Cornish boats, also, did not have the apprenticeship system for the boy learner of the crew. Hull apprentices were notoriously ill-treated. In 1882 two Hull skippers were executed for murdering apprentices. Between 1880 and 1882 no less than half the Hull apprentices contrived to get themselves in prison. They proved the truth of Samuel Johnson's famous dictum, 'No man will be a sailor who has contrivance enough to get himself into a jail; for being in a ship is being in a jail, with the chance of being drowned . . . A man in a jail has more room, better food and commonly better company.' In Grimsby too it was common for apprentices to commit offences in the hope of custodial sentences. We may be sure that in Newlyn if any boy was ill-treated at sea some formidable female member of the family would soon be around to box the skipper's ears. The family ties were very strong, whereas in Brixham, for instance, the prime source of apprentices was the orphanage and reformatory school.

In general therefore there was not only a religious difference between the Newlyn men and the East Coast people but a cultural and social one. That is not to say that Newlyn was solely inhabited by sober Methodists who never misbehaved in any way. The younger men who worked hard at sea would be likely to let off steam if they were kept ashore for any time and in any case those who are involved in hard physical labour tend to enjoy themselves rather vigorously if they have any energy left. Anything in the nature of a demonstration against hated strangers would be likely to attract them.

But was Newlyn united in the resolve to make some demonstration against the East Coast men? Certainly in later years, if not before the riots, some were not above making a little money from them, unmeshing fish when they came into harbour or mending their nets. The Cornish motto, 'One and All', is generally regarded in the county as being honoured more in the breach than the observance, but in 1830 the people of Newlyn and of Mousehole, had been firmly united in opposing any further imposition of the tithe on fish. In both villages enraged women beat up the last two men who came in an endeavour to enforce it in 1830. In Mousehole placards appeared bearing the legend 'It is better to die than to starve. No tithe. We will die first. One and All.' Newlyn was more abrupt. The inscription 'No Tithe. One and All' was placed high above the barometer in the wall of the old hostelry at the top of the slip. There it remained until 1896. Janie Kelynack records that all were not agreed about trying to stop the Sunday fishing by the East Coast men. One man realising this said 'You are no longer One and All' and pulled the board down, after which it disappeared. United or not the demonstration went ahead.

Above: Men of the Berkshire Regiment in New Road, going from Newlyn to Penzance in the period of the Riots of 1896. The two civilians with them were leading citizens of Penzance: on the officer's left, George Paulle Bazeley, J.P., and with the bicycle Sidney Godolphin Bazeley. A bicycle was at that time still an up-market form of transport. **Below**: The soldiers seem to have adopted a fairly relaxed attitude to their job of imposing virtual martial law. (*Photos: Margaret Bazeley collection*)

CHAPTER SEVEN

The Newlyn Riots

So next I tried withdrawing the men, on the mayonnaise principle, that if you don't beat the mixture it doesn't take.

(Gerard Morel, Lyon Police Superintendent)

Whether or not Newlyn men and women were unanimous in taking action over Sunday fishing on the morning of Monday, May 18th, 1896 a crowd estimated at a thousand strong assembled along the North Pier to meet the first East Coast boats coming in to discharge their catch. A dozen boats were boarded and the mackerel catch thrown into the harbour. Three boats anchored outside were boarded by men in gigs, who overwhelmed the crews and brought them into harbour in what was described as 'an open act of piracy', although no-one was ever charged for this particular incident. In all some 100,000 mackerel were thrown into the harbour, which if it achieved nothing else must have led to the gorging of every seagull for miles around. The ringleaders sent messages for help to Mousehole, Porthleven and St. Ives. The baulks were put down at Porthleven and Mousehole and a chain was stretched across The Gaps in Newlyn.

The authorities do not appear to have had any warning of the trouble which had been brewing in Newlyn, although it must have been widely talked about on doorsteps and in pubs and in other fishing communities in West Penwith. There were then no investigative journalists eager to publicise any contentious matter and interview the leading figures. The local newspapers gave full and fair reports, but they were usually retrospective. However the local civil power acted with promptness and intelligence. As Newlyn was in the county police area a message was sent to Inspector Matthews at Chyandour police station, at the east end of Penzance, a few yards outside the borough boundary. He thought it prudent to acquaint Superintendent Coombe at Camborne of the circumstances. The only speedy transport was by train and it will be recalled that there were only 219 men in the whole county to call on, so it was some hours before a strong county force could be mustered at Newlyn.

In the meantime Inspector Matthews, supported by two constables from the Penzance borough force of 13 men whose assistance he had sought, arrived on the scene. He was also accompanied by the Chief Officer of Coastguard with five men. At that time H. M. Coastguard had a very strong presence in Penzance. Their buildings, with an ornate tower, still stand in Chyandour, while in Newlyn the present Post Office on The Strand was a Coastguard house for the rocket waggon. Its origin is indicated by a granite stone, with a foul anchor symbol inscribed on it, let into the ground outside.

At this period the coastguard functioned under the Admiralty as a Naval Reserve and carried out a miscellany of nautical duties, some administrative, some connected with wreck and lifesaving and some a hangover from smuggling days. Their local influence and status was considerable and the Chief Officer attempted to intervene in the commotion at Newlyn. After a scuffle he was robbed of his authority by being laid firmly in the bottom of a punt and requested not to interfere. At this point the small force of law and order saw that there was little hope of dispersing the crowd and little further action was taken.

With few enemies available the crowd had run out of objectives and showed no inclination to indulge in mindless mayhem and destruction of property, apart from mackerel catches. A magistrate, Major Ross, accompanied by the clerk to the West Penwith magistrates, W. H. Borlase, arrived on the scene, but as tension had eased it was decided that nothing would be achieved by a reading of the Riot Act. This was despite a fracas at the Union Inn at midday, which led to the closing of the public houses. In this incident George Reynolds, master of *Warrior*, LT425, was beaten up. The authorities were well aware, however, that a great potential remained for much more serious trouble with Newlyn in its present mood. It was estimated that there were a hundred East Coast boats still at sea. If they came into the bay and if reinforcements for Newlyn arrived from St. Ives and Porthleven there were the makings of a sea-fight or a pitched battle on shore which could not be contained with the small forces available. Accordingly the Harbour Master of Newlyn, William Strick, was despatched in the steam launch *Nora* to warn off the East Coast fleet. The Customs cutter *Neptune* was sent on the same mission. The unfortunate Strick is said to have needed an escort on his return, but the East Coast men seem to have taken advice. Meanwhile supporters for Newlyn arrived from Porthleven.

The afternoon and evening of the first day passed off fairly quietly. A crowd rushed to Penzance harbour to meet an East Coat boat but she had loaded ice and departed before their arrival. Later Hobson & Sons', the Lowestoft merchants, wooden kiosk offices on the quay at Newlyn was thrown into the harbour. This appears to have been the only significant damage of its kind. There were plenty of people about all the evening, but the pubs remained closed. Several hundred stayed around until midnight. The Harbour Master was still at sea but the lugger sent in pursuit had returned, lacking the wind for an effective chase.

On Tuesday morning Inspector Matthews and P. C. Spear were injured in a scuffle at Newlyn, but when the small force of police drew their truncheons the incident fizzled out. So far the riots had been moderately well-conducted. The real trouble came on the Tuesday afternoon. Six East Coast boats were seen making for Penzance harbour and two or three hundred rioters hurried towards Penzance to prevent the landing of their fish. As they approached the harbour they were met by a detachment of eight Penzance borough police under the command of Superintendent Nicholas, with truncheons at the ready. The Newlyn men charged and ought to have won by sheer weight of numbers. But, truth to tell, they were a mere rabble and were repulsed by the determined police.

In reserve behind the Police was a force of irregulars. On the previous day the Mayor of Penzance had issued handbills inviting burgesses to enrol as special constables. His appeal was not without response. Cornish communities which are close together are notorious for maintaining what might be called a state of 'enjoyable animosity'. The relations between Penzance and Newlyn are enshrined in the verse:-

Penzance boys up in a tree
Looking as wisht as wisht can be,
Newlyn buccas, strong as oak,
Knocking them down at every stroke.

The Roman invaders of Britain soon discovered that the Celtic tribes were more interested in fighting each other than the common enemy. That tribal feeling persists and the Penzance men were far more interested in fighting the Newlyn men than supporting their cause against the 'foreigners'. From behind the police surged a body of men, some of whom were special constables, but the majority, pilots, sailors and other quay folk, armed with belaying pins, ice-axes, barrel staves and other weapons to hand. They charged into the Newlyn 'buccas' and turned a retreat into an ignominious rout amid the cheers and jeers of Penzance women lining the road.

The term 'bucca' for Newlyn men needs some explanation. Bucca was a left-over pagan sea spirit to whom the fishermen made a small offering from their catch. At the top of Gwavas Lane, or Church Lane, leading from Newlyn up to Paul, was a grassy bank, commanding a view of the bay and the encircling hills, known as The Cross. Two large rocks surmounted the bank, overhung by a hawthorn tree. According to Janie Kelynack, 'At the foot of these rocks, long ago, the fisherman placed a portion of their fish to propitiate the Bucca, the sea-god. Becoming sceptical of the efficacy of their offerings, the more venturesome watched one night and found that 'twas no spiritual being carried off their fish but human hands. From that time no more fish were offered to the Bucca.' Perhaps through this neglect Bucca was obviously not on the side of the Newlyn men when the Penzance boys put them to flight with their cudgels. And more dangerously armed opponents were already on their way.

The authorities had wisely decided that the situation might well get much worse, especially with the arrival of the St. Ives fleet later in the day. Troops were sent for and shortly before six o'clock on the Tuesday evening 330 redcoats of the Second Battalion, the Royal Berkshire Regiment, under the command of Lt. Colonel Hasard, arrived at Penzance railway station. They were met by the Chief Constable of Cornwall, Col. Walter Raleigh Gilbert, and the Justices of the Peace. A tremendous crowd gathered. Few had ever seen a soldier in the district, let alone a battalion. There had not been such excitement since another day in May, in the year 1648, when the Parliamentary forces suppressed a Royalist rising in the town and 'exquisitely plundered' it, to use the unfortunate inhabitants' own words. The sight of the Berkshires reassured them that the men of Newlyn would be restrained from anything very 'exquisite' on this occasion. A very large crowd followed the soldiers to their temporary barracks, the old Serpentine Works at Wherry town.

On the same day the Royal Navy sent three ships to the Bay, H.M.S. *Ferret*, a torpedo-boat-destroyer, as the term then was, H.M.S. *Traveller*, a special service vessel, and H.M.S. *Curlew*, a gunboat tender to H.M.S. Cambridge. Commander C. P. Ogle, R.N., was the senior officer, and an armed party of one warrant officer, three petty officers and twenty seamen was formed.

The people of Newlyn were not browbeaten by the arrival of the military and in the evening something of a pitched battle took place near the Lareggan river at Wherrytown. On the one side were Newlyn and Porthleven fishermen, now backed by the men of St. Ives, whose fleet is said to have looked like an armada as it arrived in Mount's Bay, with pennants flying. On the other side were East Coat men, supported by Penzance people. Sticks, stones and fists were used and a strong force of nearly a hundred police, under Superintendents Coombe and Bassett, became a target and were unable to contain the riot. The troops were called and made a sufficient show of strength to break up the fighting. They marched on Newlyn, accompanied by several hundred Penzance people, eager to see their neighbours under military occupation. Officers used the flats of their swords on any who would not give way and it is reported that in a subsequent disturbance an officer cut off a man's ear with his sword. Thus something not far removed from martial law was established, with soldiers on the quays and patrolling the streets, road blocks set up and a strong force of police still in evidence.

The sight of the armed soldiers in the village and the warships in the bay persuaded the Newlyn men that the authorities would not tolerate any further disorder; but they would not go to sea and affirmed their views on Sunday fishing even if God appeared to be on the side of the big battalions.

There was only one further disturbance of note, when on the Wednesday evening a body of Penzance youths marched to Newlyn. Stones were thrown, windows broken and the military called. The road to Newlyn was then sealed off at the western end of Penzance promedade.

Although there were a number of professional photographers

active in the district at the time no photographs of the disturbance have come to light. One photographer, H. Gartrell, did attempt to take some photographs of the riots, but his negatives were seized and spoilt as 'the men did not want it to be made known in the papers'. 'White-collar' sight-seers in Newlyn were also roughly handled. There was little sympathy for those who thought the defence of Newlyn's livelihood a mere source of entertainment.

However, by the Thursday, May 21st, the fighting had stopped and the talking had commenced. The troops, who had been received with defiance, catcalls and jeers, settled in. British servicemen have long had a remarkable talent for public relations, when so minded. Somehow they manage by their attitude to gain the respect of the local population. As ordinary people they sympathise with other ordinary people and especially those with an even less comfortable life-style than their own. Not for them the gibe against the American GI's of being 'over-paid, over-fed, over-sexed and over here'. In Newlyn the Berkshires gained the confidence of the people in a very short time and no doubt lent a sympathetic ear to their grievance which we can be sure they were informed of at some length.

It was all over, bar the shouting. Telegrams began to fly and the Fishermen's Committee Chairman Joseph Pascoe, issued a lengthy statement.

The Lowestoft fishing vessel *Chamois LT 303* running for Newlyn in heavy seas. In similar circumstances the Newlyn lugger *Jane* was lost running dead before the wind towards Penzance harbour on October 7th, 1880. (*Photo: Reg Watkiss collection*)

Two Newlyn fishermen circa 1900. The one on the right is undoubtedly retired! (*Photo: Reg Watkiss collection*)

CHAPTER EIGHT

Justice and Arbitration

The Riots are done with and forgotten now, the only remainder of a dead volcano being the presence in the roads of H.M.S. Spanker, *and even that is by common consent attributed to the presence of French crabbers at the Seven Stones.*

(F. G. Aflalo in *The Sea Fishing Industry*, 1904)

The statement by the Fishermen's Committee was directed at the Home Secretary and was published at length in the *Cornish Telegraph*. A telegram was sent to the Home Secretary, asking him to receive a delegation, and also to McArthur, M.P. for the St. Austell division of Cornwall, asking him to use his influence. In the course of the riots, Bedford Bolitho, M.P, had talked to a delegation and also to the men in Newlyn. Having been prominent in the promotion of the new harbour he had influence with them, but he failed to restrain them and was reported to have been unsympathetic on the subject of their working hours. Subsequently in a letter to the *Cornish Telegraph* he denied this, saying that he supported the men's case, but not their methods. In a leader the newspaper chided the men for their action in the terms usual on such occasions. While it was agreed that Sunday fishing was not permitted in Scottish or Irish waters, and that was a strong point, the fishermen had no proper representative organisation, had forfeited sympathy and had little prospect of legislative help.

The Fishermen's Committee statement was an articulate document. If the standard of education in Newlyn was not high it did at least enable people to express themselves in clear English, an ability helped in no small measure by the fact that they listened to passages from the Authorised Version of the Bible every Sunday in chapel. But in the document they did not hesitate to state the commercial advantages of maintaining the Sabbath. Economically they felt themselves too hard-pressed to do otherwise. The statement appeared in the *Cornish Telegraph* on the Thursday, May 21st.

'In the first place we have received from our ancestors the blessing of the Sabbath Day, and believe that if the Sabbath is kept it will be better for us not only in the religious but in a pecuniary sense; we believe it is best for the Lowestoft men and for ourselves that there should be no fishing on Sundays; and that there should be a clear market on Monday morning. This grievance began some thirty years ago. The agitation was partly carried out by the St. Ives men but did not quite succeed. About eighteen years ago they succeeded in putting down fishing on the Sabbath, and we, believing that it was for the benefit of all that the Sabbath should be prohibited, have been trying through our leading men, by influence and all other lawful ways, to succeed. Now we have been driven to this, and this is the only way we can bring our grievances before the public. Our great point is that it would be better for us from a money standpoint to desist from Sunday fishing and to have a clear market on the Monday. Lowestoft men go to sea night after night, and they get in on the Monday morning with their fish in a very decomposed state, so as not to be fit for human food; they spoil the market and there is no chance of prices rising again for the whole week. The unwritten law or custom of this port is that everyone shall stop fishing from Friday night until Monday night, so that the markets may have a chance to clear themselves and the fish are then in a better condition, and prices are kept up through the whole week. What has irritated us is that the Lowestoft fishermen have made a statement that they will have our harbour, have our homes, and that they will take our wives. That is their fond boast. We are not fighting with an isolated case. The Irishmen the Scotchman and the Cornishmen all desist from fishing on a Sunday. Lowestoft and Yarmouth are the only two ports that we are fighting. It is not the United Kingdom but these two places which are destroying our livelihood.

And now what we want is not that the East Coast boats shall be kept from fishing among us. We will give them the right hand of fellowship. Let them come and fish, but they must abide by the custom of the Port, and if they will not conform we are determined, cost what it will, that we will fight to the bitter end. The Lowestoft men have said scores of times that they would be glad to have the Sunday, but owing to the pressure put upon them by their owners they cannot do as they wish. They have expressed themselves as being no more than brute creation dogs. It is also advisable to have the Sabbath day free for the sake of the craft which want cleaning up and putting in order. As an instance of how the Lowestoft men glut the market, it may be stated that when we, the Cornishmen, returned with our fish after the Monday night they fetched 4s. (20p) instead of 14s (70p) a hundred. Our grievance is that Sunday morning takes from us our bread and butter, and we would rather die in the struggle than that our children should run the risk of starvation. It is not so much with some of us a matter of keeping the Sabbath, but we want to keep the market healthy.'

Besides the statement there was much talk of a deputation to London and of a thousand true Cornishmen at the door of the House of Commons singing 'Shall Trelawny die?'. In the event the deputation sent on Saturday, May 23rd, consisted of Messrs. Pascoe, Batten, Humphreys and Rogers. The Home Secretary refused to receive them and two weeks later made a statement rejecting the Newlyn case. As he did so two more warships, H.M.S. *Banshee* and H.M.S. *Opossum*, were sent to Mount's Bay as a precaution, and the ships which had been previously there were also put on alert.

The East Coast men were equally unimpressed by Newlyn's protest. A skipper in Plymouth stated that it was fortunate that the whole East Coast fleet of 500 boats with 8,000 men did not put into Newlyn to take vengeance. Their case was that, excepting the skipper and mate, the crew were paid a weekly wage and had to proceed to sea whenever ordered. To stop fishing on certain days of the week would mean absolute ruin to owners and crew.

To represent the interests of the East Coast owners R. B. Capps, of Capps Bros., went to stay at the Queen's Hotel, Penzance. He was particularly incensed because during the disturbances someone had tried to run down his son in a launch. On behalf of his fellow owners he was demanding £800 in damages from Newlyn.

On Tuesday, May 26th the main body of the Royal Berkshires departed from Penzance station, to the plaudits of the Penzance people who had seen them quell the Newlyn buccas. On the following day Penzance borough council met in secret session, under Mayor W. J. Bazeley. The result of its deliberations were not too secret. The *Cornish Telegraph* 'understood' that the Council had resolved to offer harbour facilities to East Coast boats until the end of the season.

This opportunist move was approved of in Penzance and bitterly resented in Newlyn as being a swift stab in the back. 'The right hand of fellowship', promised by Mayor Julyan at the opening of the North Pier, two years before, had been re-deployed. Councillors said, virtuously, that Cornish sympathies had been alienated by the 'riotous conduct'.

The Newlyn men turned back waggons with Penzance tradesmen's goods in reprisal and said that they would boycott Penzance shops and start a co-operative store. Mousehole people were equally indignant. They gained the nickname of Mousehole 'Cut-throats', because they swore that they would slit the throats of the East Coast men.

Amid all this activity in the wake of the riots the action of the local magistrate remains the most curious – curious because like Sherlock Holmes famous dog in the night, they did nothing, at least for some time. During all the disturbance not a man had been arrested, charged or even subsequently issued with a summons. The reason may have been purely practical. In the melées the police did not have sufficient force to seize and hold anyone, or vans into which prisoners could be hustled and removed from the scene. Nevertheless the ringleaders were well-known and could have been subsequently taken in charge. A bench of English landowners at that time would almost certainly have been fierce in their reprisals. A Cornish bench took a milder view. The Celtic sense of community was stronger, the gentry less feudal in outlook. Indeed there were few landed justices as West Cornwall did not have many large scale resident land-owners. Victorian class divisions certainly existed but autocracy was not easily tolerated. Two stories illustrate this feeling. Many years ago Colonel Edward (later Sir Edward) Bolitho was Master of the Western Hunt. MFH's in the field are notoriously impatient in the conduct of their business and on one occasion the colonel came cantering up to a gate beside which an old Cornishman stood. The old man made no move to extend the usual courtesy of opening the gate for a horseman. 'Open the bloody gate man, open the gate!', roared the Colonel. 'You want the gate open, open the bloody gate yourself, 'oo the 'ell do you think you are, B'litha?', was the only response. The Colonel spluttered, but rose to the occasion. 'Quite right, quite right, that's what I call a man.' The same sort of feeling inspired some casual farm workers who disapproved of the farmer coming round haughtily on horseback to give his orders. Accordingly they enlarged a ditch where he customarily came over the hedge. He fell into the field with a satisfactory loss of dignity.

The magistrates, however, were not only reluctant to proceed from a sense of community. They feared the consequence of issuing summonses. A thousand men had at one stage been involved in rioting and there were at that time about double that number of fishermen in the district. The police themelves were apprehensive about going into Newlyn and singling out individuals. Only a detachment of the Berkshires had been left behind in case of further trouble and the action of Penzance Town Council had not improved feelings in Newlyn. In the end they had no choice. The Home Secretary took the justifiable view that such large scale disturbances, with all the measures required to quell them, could not be allowed to pass off without consequential prosecutions.

Eventually ten summonses were served in Newlyn and, to everyone's relief, without incident. At the beginning of June the men appeared before the magistrates in Penzance, who were C. C. Ross (Chairman), T. R. Bolitho, E. L. Millett, J. R. Branwell, J. Corin, H. Laity, G. P. Bazeley, T. W. Field and Major Ross. The hearing lasted four days and, judging by the absence of public interest after the first day, was tedious. One man was discharged and nine were committed for trial at the County Assizes, charged mainly with rioting and riotous assembly. The men were Thomas Hosking, Nicholas Paul Hosking, J. G. Richards, William Tonkin, George Glasson, William Mann, William Triggs, Alfred and Thomas Harvey. In a sense these men were scapegoats. As the riots could be ascribed to the inspiration of the Fishermen's Committee it would have been normal to hold such a body responsible. It had been decided not to charge any of them, another symptom of the authorities' forbearance, or nervousness.

Nevertheless when justice was done it was, by modern standards, extraordinarily swift. Fortunately the Assizes were due and the authorities obviously wanted the matter done rather than smouldering away. The men appeared at Bodmin Assizes, before Mr. Justice Lawrence, on June 13th.

The trial was equally swift. The jury acquitted one Harvey and recommended Green and Hosking to mercy. The remainder were all found guilty and remanded until the Monday to appear for sentence, all but one of them on bail. The judge then sentenced them all to be bound over for twelve months to keep the peace. He said that the prisoners had to thank counsel on both sides for the lenient treatment which they had received.

On their return the men were received by a quiet crowd at Penzance station but in Newlyn there was an enthusiastic reception, with bunting and a band playing. However, the men, who had probably been the recipients of strong advice, went quietly to their homes and did not seek 'lionisation'. They had not become martyrs. Mr. Justice Lawrence must have been a man of remarkably liberal inclinations for his time. But it was no secret that a great deal of backstage consultation had gone on in relation to the treatment of the rioters. Bedford Bolitho was no doubt active and it was known that Canon Carah, a former curate of St. Peter's in Newlyn, had been influential. The Judge did not escape criticism of his sentencing policy from other quarters, but it proved correct.

There was no further violence, but what, in effect, were no more than echoes of the affair rumbled on for a year or so, with some minor incidents when Cornish boats were on the East Coast in the autumn. The Home Secretary had refused to support the Newlyn case, as there was no illegality in Sunday fishing, whatever 'the custom of the port' might be.

When the riots were first heard about in East Anglia, by telegram on the Monday, May 18th, 'deep indignation' was felt in Lowestoft. A meeting of the Boatowners' Protection Society was called at once. The Chairman, Councillor W. F. Rice and Councillor A. B. Capps, the Secretary, were despatched to Newlyn, via a meeting with their local M.P. at Westminster. The following Saturday the *Lowestoft Journal* reported the events at Newlyn in remarkably similar terms to those of the Cornish papers. Either they used a Cornish reporter as a correspondent or they indulged in the time-honoured practice of 'lifting' another newspaper's report. In any case the reports were restrained and objective, more so than might be the case to-day. The *Lowestoft Journal* did not, however, fail to make the observation that the Cornish custom of not fishing on Sundays was 'not entirely due as an act of obedience to the Fourth Commandment'. They knew well in East Anglia that it was the Monday market that the Cornish were more concerned with. And they also commented that the Cornish fishermen were 'less energetic' than their East Anglian counterparts and viewed their rivals' success 'with jealousy'.

The East Anglians were certainly exercised by the fact that while there was a legal remedy for riot damage on shore, vessels were not covered by the statutes and there was probably little hope of their being so. It seemed to them a poor deal that while there was no illegality in their Sunday fishing, there was no way of extracting compensation from the Newlyn men for their illegal acts.

Nevertheless the Board of Trade was bound to effect some conciliation and recompense. Their arbitrator made an award of £619 to the East Coast owners, skippers and crews in relation to the loss they had suffered in the riots. In that it was not the result of a court action this award had no legal force. Nevertheless it was accepted and Bedford Bolitho agreed to be personally responsible for its payment.

This helped to make an amicable start to a conference between the two sides held in the House of Commons in January 1897, under the Chairmanship of A. D. Berrington, Inspector of Fisheries. Bedford Bolitho led the Cornish delegation, while the East Coast interest was led by H. S. Foster, M.P., his opposite number. The latter expressed his approval that the religious aspect of the dispute had been disclaimed and that the argument was now purely commercial. The Cornish wanted a ban on fishing on Saturday and Sunday nights. The East Coast men, after initial disunity on the issue wanted no restriction on the grounds that it would be too damaging commercially. One of the owners, Capps, made the point that the East Coast ketches were bigger, better, faster and had superior tackle. The corollary of that was that the owners' boats were more capital intensive and hence must be earning on as many days and nights in the year as possible. Berrington, who must have found his task a taxing one, produced the inevitable compromise suggestion – that there should be no fishing on Saturday nights. Both sides went away to think about this and the idea was eventually accepted – at least nominally. A further joint meeting was held in Newlyn in the following April, with the ever-patient Bedford Bolitho in the chair. Again the meeting started amicably. But fishing agreements or regulations are notoriously difficult to police. They remain so today, despite every modern form of surveillance, expensively deployed. It even seems impossible to convince the authorities that a trawler catching pelagic fish can be mid-water trawling and not bottom trawling!

In 1897 Newlyn men were not convinced that East Coast boats which did not come into port on a Saturday night were not quietly fishing. The Fishery Protection Service was then in being, but had no obligation to enforce what was only a gentleman's agreement. Thanks to a Newlyn hothead the East Coast men walked out of the meeting. They had agreed among themselves to keep out of Newlyn as much as possible that year and use Penzance and Plymouth instead.

In due course the subject of Sunday fishing faded as a major issue. Writing in his *Sea Fishing Industry of England and Wales*, F. G. Aflalo remarked, 'The Riots are practically forgotten. On a Sunday in 1903 I found the Newlyn men themselves packing fishing and loading carts, an endless procession of which, even with the disregarded chapel bells calling worshippers to the town on the other side of the harbour, fed the quays with returned empties.'

The conclusion which must be reached on Newlyn's great protest demonstration against Sunday fishing must be that it was ill-conceived, ill-organised, ill-led and ineffective. The men did not even fight well, for they were routed in their engagements. But that is to their credit for at heart they were in the main peaceable men. Moreover Aflalo's comment must be treated with some reserve as, whatever they may have done ashore, Newlyn men persisted in not going to sea on Sundays.

Probably the day of the opening of the North Pier, 3rd July, 1894. In the foreground are nets spread to dry on The Bowjey. On the left is the building known as Factory Row, where nets and gear were made. Most of the houses in the foreground were demolished c. 1937. The photo gives a good idea of the 40-acre extent of the harbour. (*Photo: Reg Watkiss collection*)

The opening of the North Pier on July 3rd, 1894. The centre figure in top hat is Thomas Bedford Bolitho a benefactor of the port. (*Photo: Gibson*)

CHAPTER NINE

Change And Revolution

We live in an era of quiet change and revolution, and our fishermen will not longer be able quietly to follow in the footsteps of their fathers and great-grandfathers.
(E. W. Crofts in *The Cornishman*, July 26th, 1883)

F. G. Aflalo, F.R.G.S., F.Z.S., who published his *Sea Fishing Industry of England and Wales* in 1904, called the book *A Popular Account of the Sea Fisheries and Fishing Ports of Those Countries*. Few writers at that time seemed inclined to write either popular or scholarly accounts of the fishing industry in general and much the same is true now. There are any number of studies of fishing craft and specialist books on marine biology or catching methods but general accounts have always been rare. 'Popular' or not in his writings Aflalo was a perceptive student of the industry. His remarks on Penzance and Newlyn, following his visit in 1903 were shrewd indeed and to some degree prophetic.

Aflalo looked at the curious fact that although Penzance had a large harbour, with a siding from the rail terminus actually running along the Albert Pier, fish was landed at Newlyn and carted to Penzance. It seemed that nothing would induce the summer mackerel fleets, local or East Coast to land at Penzance. Aflalo's view was that Penzance Harbour looked 'exceedingly safe for children to fall into, but scarcely suited to the requirements of a fishing fleet'. To Penzance Corporation he thought the harbour was probably a white elephant and that it would be 'not unsafe to prophesy' that it would pass under the control of the Great Western Railway who would fill up one third and properly dredge the remainder. Alternatively he seemed to think that the G.W.R. might have profitably run a light railway around the bay to Newlyn. This was an idea which appeared briefly again in the thirties. At any rate Aflalo's prophecy in relation to Penzance harbour proved unsound. He over-looked the evidence that the railway company was not primarily interested in the fish trade from West Cornwall. The memory of the Great Western Railway receives great veneration in the West Country. Indeed there can be few industrial organisations which commanded such loyalty in their lifetime and such adulation after their demise. Employee loyalty is displayed on a tombstone in Penzance cemetery with the words 'late GWR' inscribed with as much pride as if the deceased had served in a famous regiment. But it must be confessed that the company failed Newlyn to a considerable degree. A writer in *The Cornishman* complained that the G.W.R., with its monopoly of transport, charged £5 per ton for the carriage of fish, compared with 15s 11d (80p) for ordinary goods. 'It would', he wrote, 'be useless to appeal to the better feelings of the Railway Company, for they appear to have none.' Whether or not they had better feelings the G.W.R. undoubtedly had some feelings. In 1900 a leading railway writer, W. M. Acworth, defended the policy of the railways generally in relation to the fish trade. He pointed out that fish was a perishable traffic peculiarly difficult to work. It came in fits and starts according to the volume of landings, yet the rolling stock must be ready on the instant. There was the problem of returned fish boxes which was undoubtedly a major logistical headache.

Acworth argued that if herrings were undoubtedly cheap at Lowestoft and comparatively dear in London much the same applied to Newcastle coal but no-one suggested that the railways should carry it at loss. Involved calculations of charges and comparisons were indulged in without enabling the reader to reach any very firm conclusions and the author himself had to confess that the fixed and published railway charges were the only element of certainty in the whole calculation. Aflalo, for his part on the subject, joined issue on the vexed question of ordinary fish rates and rates for fish sent at owners' risk.

The G.W.R. would, no doubt, have produced all sorts of figures justifying its scale of charges for the carriage of fish from Penzance. By the same token it would also have produced reasons for not wishing to make a capital investment in the development of the harbour at Penzance for fish landing, despite the adjacent position of the terminus and the existing siding on the Albert Pier. But other railways, in other parts of the country, had thought differently in relation to the fish trade. Notably, the Great Eastern Railway Company had developed the harbour at Lowestoft, and the Great Central Railway had done the same at Grimsby, while the docks at Hull were also very much a railway creation.

The Great Western itself was responsible for the development of Milford Haven as a fishing port. The tonnage landed there increased from 9,398 tons in 1890 to 24,100 tons in 1902. The fish train left Milford each day at 1600 and arrived in Paddington at 0230 the next morning. In the period 1890 to 1902 the population of Milford Haven doubled to 6,500. Ironically, Milford, which was mainly a trawler port, received a boost in 1902, when two Newlyn boats landed mackerel at its 1,000 ft long fish quay. It is hard to escape the suspicion that, while west Wales was too remote for tourists, the G.W.R. saw Penzance and Cornwall generally, mainly in terms of passenger traffic. The company originally had its sights fixed on the port of Falmouth, which began to decline in general importance. Paddington was notably never short of publicity ideas and someone found that a map of Italy in mirror image was very like the outline of Cornwall. The idea of 'The Cornish Riviera' was born. By 1892 there was 'The Cornishman' express passenger train, which by 1896 had to be run in two parts in the summer months. In 1904 the 'Cornish Riviera Express Limited' was inaugurated, 'The Riv,' of happy memory, terminating at Penzance. The acid comment has been provoked that obviously the Great Western preferred clean tourists to smelly fish, but that now we think the fish clean and the tourists smelly.

While the Lowestoft men saw the advantages of using Penzance harbour, Penzance town council, after its initial move to encourage them at the time of riots, devised no long term policy. In the coming years the town's base in relation to mining, smelting the port, and local industry generally was to decline. The town council, despite the presence of businessmen on it, who were successful in their own right, never developed a proper strategy for the town's economic future. The tourist trade began to take the place of industry on an opportunity basis. Now, a century on from the peak of Penzance's industrial prosperity, there are ominous signs of economic crisis and only a recent appearance of agreed economic strategy in the plans for the re-development of the harbour area.

When in 1904 Aflalo posed the idea of filling in a third of the tidal part of the harbour at Penzance to form a fish market with direct rail connection, he foresaw that the railways had reason to fear future competition from road vehicles. In 1968 Penzance borough council did cause a third of the harbour to be filled with quarry waste, but not for the purpose Aflalo suggested. A very large car park was created. It must have seemed a good idea at the time, but, at a stroke, it compounded the acute traffic circulation problems from which the town suffers, and is a potential source of delay for fish lorries.

In the case of the harbour at Newlyn, Aflalo saw that facilities were inadequate at the height of the mackerel season and advocated the building of a pier, with landing facilities on either side, right in the centre of the harbour. Newlyn had to wait until the 1970's for such a pier.

Within a few years of the riots the Cornish fishermen had to face even more competition from the East Coast, which turned to the steam drifter with great rapidity. On his Sunday visit in 1903, Aflalo averred that East Coast steam drifters had landed their catch but that the Cornish fleet was still at sea, contending with contrary winds.

After the riots life continued in Newlyn and in the fishing industry much as before. They had changed nothing and could be dismissed as an ineffective demonstration, which had fortunately passed off with a minimum of serious consequences. And yet, coming when they did, they marked the end of the old ways, and, in the way that events cast their shadow before them, ushered in the profound changes in attitudes and life-style which were to characterise the next century with its global upheavals and immense advances in technology.

A journal by William Williams of life and events in Newlyn, now lodged in the Penzance Library spanned the period from 1771 to 1836, nearly a man's lifetime. In those years the journal shows that hardly anything in the village changed at all. True, the long French wars ceased, but their effect on local communities was mainly peripheral. In Cornwall the main effect was the end of the threat of the press gang and the diversion of naval resources to the suppression of smuggling. If William Williams had come back in 1880 however he would have found two principal changes: the increased size and improved design of boats, enabling them to venture around the coast of the British Isles, and the presence of the railway connection. He would have been pleased by the access to up-country markets, less pleased with the presence of fishermen from other parts of the country. In general he could have resumed his life and occupation without much mental adjustment from his life a hundred years before.

It is hardly necessary to say that if William Williams had suffered another reincarnation in 1980 the changes would have been beyond his imagination, just as those for the year 2080 A.D. may be beyond ours. Even by 1896 the speed of change had begun to accelerate. Powered fishing vessels had arrived in force, even if there were not yet many in the West Country. The international scene at sea was being darkened by the armaments race. Between 1895 and 1903 Britain doubled her number of first-class battleships and Germany quadrupled hers. For Newlyn the significance of this came on the first Sunday of August 1914 when hundreds of men of the Royal Naval Reserve mustered on the Quay at Penzance and marched to the railway station to entrain for the naval barracks and be assigned to their ships. It is recorded that 'as the train left the Station a mighty cheer burst from the thousands who were watching'. The first global event to affect Newlyn's life and work in the 20th century had begun. By November 11th 1918 there were seventy two names of those who died to be placed on the war memorial on the Strand. The granite memorial is by local stone worker Arnold Snell and the striking copper relief of marching men by Merrifield. One may look on the long list of names on the memorial but more poignant is to hear the Roll of Honour called at Paul Church, which includes Mousehole men, and is solemnly read on Remembrance Sunday every year. For the First World War the list goes alphabetically, on and on and on, so that by the time the letter 'm' is reached one wonders when it will end. The grief it represents is unimaginable, particularly as many Newlyn and Mousehole families were intermarried. A generation of the youngest and fittest fishermen was decimated.

For those who stayed and continued fishing there was a convoy system to the mackerel grounds, in company with the 'Yorkies', East Coast fishermen, and escorted by the armed Yarmouth drifter *C & E W*, armed with a 3-pounder gun. This vessel also went with the pilchard fleet to the Wolf grounds in the autumn. In the First World War U-boats were active in coastal waters and sank many small craft. Counter measures in Mount's Bay consisted of a seaplane base on the shore by Penlee Quarry and an airship base at Mullion. Further away, but in a position to protect Newlyn, was another seaplane base, adjacent to New Grimsby harbour on the island of Tresco in Scilly.

The impact of the outside world on Newlyn at the beginning of the century was traumatic enough and was to be followed by the general economic depression of the twenties and thirties. But Cornwall's economy as a county was in itself in decline. In the eighteen-nineties the collapse in the price of tin, to be repeated dramatically less than a century later, led to widespread emigration. And the mining district of St. Just no longer provided a source of casual labouring employment in bad fishing times. Cornwall was already on the long road of de-industrialisation which by the mid-nineteen-eighties was to leave fishing as one of the few productive industries, as opposed to service industries and tourism.

One effect of the war was to rest the fishing grounds so that for the immediate post-war period stocks were good. But while the long-term outlook might have appeared to be good, advance in technology soon led to very significant declines and the elimination of traditional fisheries.

In Falmouth harbour there is a small, but locally important oyster fishery, carried out by small sailing craft towing dredges capable of being hauled manually by one man. In recent years it has been much subjected to a disease of oysters which found its way from France. However, the limited area of beds in the upper part of Falmouth Haven has been successfully conserved for many years by a simple, enforceable measure. No power, other than sail or kedging may be used. It could be argued, although the point is highly academic, that if by an extraordinary international agreement the use of power for sea-fishing had always been banned there would be little to worry about over fish stocks today. But power came and it came to stay. When all the world's fishing fleets relied on sail and oar their effectiveness was naturally limited by weather; too much wind, too little wind, sea-state, foul tide and radius of action in relation to economic size and so forth. Power changed all that. Even before it was used for propulsion it was installed for hauling gear, enabling heavier cable to be handled.

As far as Newlyn was concerned their East Coast competitors started with immediate advantages. Their sailing vessels were already larger than their Cornish counterparts. The company owners had greater resources of finance and technology to build even larger steam drifters in which boiler room and machinery space took up one third of the waterline length. Under the Cornish system of ownership there was simply not the capital available to build vessels which were so expensive in terms of first cost and non-earning space. On the East Coast the adoption of steam power accelerated at great speed. Lowestoft built its first steam drifter in 1898. By 1905 there were 101 and by 1909 the total was 243. Newlyn did not get its first steam drifter until 1908, the *Speedwell*, and she did not set a trend. The East Coast ports were handier to the Midland and Yorkshire coalfields, while the nearest major source for West Cornwall was the South Wales field. Its steam coal was ideal, but the transport cost, by sea or rail, was high. The Cornish mines imported it for their massive beam engines because they had no choice.

The benefits of power only really came to the Cornish fishermen with the internal combustion engine, at first in the form of the small petrol/paraffin engine. It was started and stopped on petrol, but ran on the cheaper paraffin. It was more fuel-efficient than steam, occupied less space, and didn't need the employment of a stoker. It was the answer for Cornwall. Much pioneer work in the development of the marine petrol engine had been carried out by the Royal National Lifeboat Institution as early as 1904. Remarkably, considering the state of the art in motor-car engines at that date, an engine was produced which satisfied the exacting requirements for lifeboats. A decade later, surprisingly in the middle of the First World War, the first internal combustion engines began to appear in Mount's Bay boats in the shape of 26 h.p. and 36 h.p. Kelvin engines. Early boats with engines were *Ben MacChree*, *Edgar*, *Hopeful*, *Boy Willy*, *Our Lizzie* and *Nellie Jane*. The first pilchard-driver to have an engine made do with a 7-h.p. Kelvin. Johnny Hosking's *Breadwinner* was the first mackerel driver to have an auxiliary. Two boats were ambitious enough to have semi-diesels, *Emblem* before 1916, and *Ben MacChree* also had a Bollinder semi-diesel. For some reason development of small marine diesels lagged until after the Second World War. In the 1950's the semi-diesel was still in employment and at this period even the R.N.L.I. had lagged in the introduction of diesels.

In terms of horsepower all the early engines were small. The *Nellie Jane* at 52ft in length by 16ft beam was the largest mackerel driver in the bay and was equipped with two 26 h.p. Kelvins, which gave her a service speed of six knots. A similar vessel today would be equipped with a 250 h.p diesel. If a boat had one engine installed the propeller was located on an A-bracket on the port quarter, which took account of the nets being shot on the starboard side. Later it became popular practice to have a main engine and a second, smaller 'wing' engine for use in case of failure. The first generation of new boats built with engines came immediately after the war, a pioneer being *Ocean Pride*, built in 1919 and still in service over sixty years later.

The fishermen had to become his own mechanic and develop a new skill in maintaining engines and carrying out repairs at sea or in distant ports where services might be expensive or non-existent. Cornishmen as a whole do not conform to any romantic notion of Celtic mysticism and a highly artistic culture. Like the Scots, their genius has shown itself most notably in engineering inventiveness and skill. Engines were therefore not a great problem. The *Nellie Jane* had Kelvin engines with two magnetos on each. When one magneto failed one day and the engine stopped the crew approached the problem by taking the wires off it and putting them on the other magneto. The engine promptly started. Inspired by this they wrote to Kelvin's suggesting that two magnetos were more trouble than one. No reply was received to this communication but no more Kelvin engines were sent out with two magnetos.

On another occasion the crew dealt with gearbox trouble in an Irish port by stripping the box and re-assembling it.

Even if the early engines were low in power the advantages of power propulsion could scarcely be doubted. Not only was there little delay in getting to and from the grounds, but either the range of trips or the number per week could be increased. Moreover the next generation of boats built for Newlyn were generally increased in length to about 50ft. Newlyn men could now put to sea in adverse southerly winds which would have kept the sailing luggers pinned in harbour. St. Ives, on the north coast had lost its old advantage. A new era had indeed begun, but a severe debit side soon began to show up.

A Newlyn woman fish jouster with her donkey shay (chaise). The grooming of the donkey has been neglected. (*Photo: Richards Collection, The Penzance Library*)

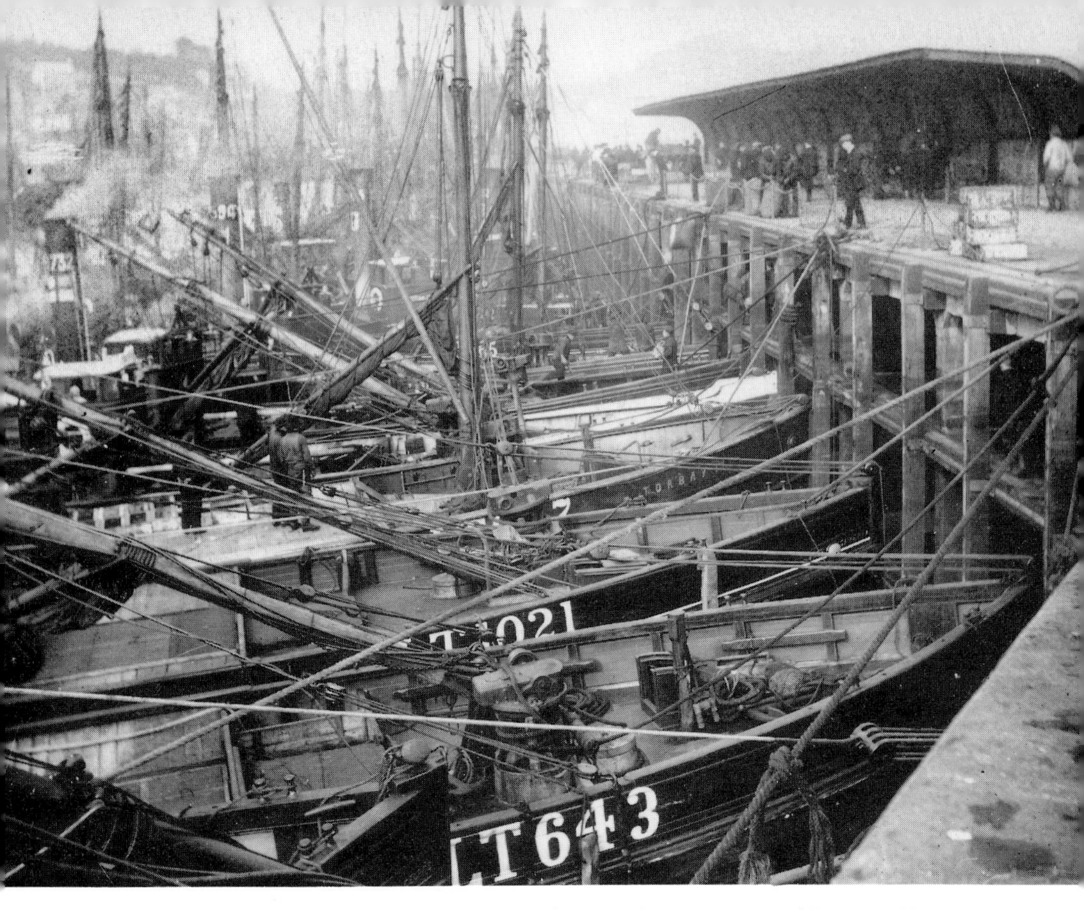

Lowestoft steam drifters in Newlyn for mackerel in 1935 (*Photo: Richards Collection, The Penzance Library)*

CHAPTER TEN

Where Have All The Fishes Gone?

They that spread nets upon the waters shall languish.
(Isiah 19:8)

After the First World War the traditional fishing seasons based on Newlyn seemed undisturbed, but in the next two decades there came severe changes. They were to be succeeded by a second series after the Second World War, a series still in the process of unfolding.

When it comes to recording the reasons for the decline of any particular fishery one is immediately met with several schools of thought. Convincing arguments are produced for what people wish to believe, which is not to say that the arguments are necessarily invalid. The scientists must be presumed to be entirely objective, although this does not ensure their views being accepted or right. Apart from the scientists, some will say that the end of a fishery and the virtual disappearance of stocks has been caused by simple overfishing and/or the destruction of breeding grounds. This will be ascribed to pressure on stocks by ever larger and more efficient power vessels, with more powerful hauling gear, modern navigational aids, and ever-improving fish detection equipment. Add to this the use of highly effective netting methods, the destruction of breeding grounds, an element of foreign competition and the difficulty of policing the fisheries and that particular school of thought feels no need to look any further.

In relation to particular species there are, however, other views which may be advanced. The appearance and disappearance of certain stocks may be caused by changes in oceanic water temperatures, or, suggest the scientists, a change in phosphate content. There is yet another argument. The fishery may have declined, although the stock are still there, but change in public taste or foreign competition make fishing no longer economic. Anyone who lives in a fishing port and wishes for a quiet life does well not to take sides in any of these arguments. The argument will always remain because while the effect of farming on the landscape is plain to see, the seascape is largely impenetrable. We may measure, calculate, analyse and make all kinds of observations, but lack any comprehensive view of what is going on beneath the surface of the ocean. A satellite may give quite a clear picture of the weather pattern, there is nothing comparable for the large scale movement of fish.

This is not to say that there is any lack of circumstantial evidence about the decline of certain stocks. As far as Newlyn and Cornwall in general were concerned the first fishery to disappear, and in a very short period, was the herring. Until a study was undertaken in the Firth of Forth in 1862 there was no scientific knowledge of the breeding habits of any commercial fish. Perhaps the simplest fact is that the eggs of all commercial fish float, except those of the herring, the spawn of which adhere to stones and weed on the seabed. This fish has two spawning periods, one promoting the summer fishery and one the winter and spring fishery.

In relation to Cornwall there were two groups of herring, those in Mount's Bay and north of St. Ives and West Cornwall and those which spawned in Bigbury Bay in South Devon and were of a smaller size. The local fisherman of Bigbury Bay caught turbot and ray on lines and it is said that the Plymouth trawlers heard of this and went a-trawling with sprat cod-ends fitted on the trawls, ruining the spawning grounds, where half-spent and spent herrings were caught. That was the end of the Bigbury Bay herrings.

The herrings of the north coast of Cornwall, which appeared first each year on Hayle Bar and Padstow Bar came from the Smalls spawning grounds off south-west Wales. The French trawlers came to work these grounds and that was the end of those herrings.

When the 1932–33 Plymouth herring season came along boats found themselves in debt and unable to pay for fuel. A decade later it was reported that the collapse of the herring fishery had caused distress in Cornwall and that this, combined with poor years for pilchards had caused 50% of most Cornish fishing fleets to be sold off since 1918. In those days share fishermen did not qualify for the dole if bad weather prevented them from fishing.

There were still herrings to be caught in the North Sea and northern waters and some Cornishmen still went to the north for them. Big fleets still operated. In the year 1931, Jack Worth, of Mousehole counted 327 drifters in Stornoway in the Outer Hebrides. By the mid 1970's the herring was nearing total extinction as a species and a complete ban on herring fishing was imposed. The finest herring were reputed to come from just west of Barra at the south end of the Outer Hebridean chain. On a visit about that time the author discovered that probably for the first time in history not a herring was to be seen in Barra's harbour. The great fishery, which altered the balance of trade in Europe in medieval times when the herring left the Baltic, was no more. By the time stocks had revived sufficiently for a limited catch to be permitted the British public, by now largely conditioned to fish fingers from supermarkets, had lost its taste for herrings. It may well be that there are again seasonal herring stocks off Cornwall, but the market is very small.

As the herring fishery declined so did the traditional mackerel fishery, although in various other ways it has lasted until the present time. Until 1924 it remained the principal fishery for Cornwall and Newlyn. There were 400 first-class Cornish boats and some 200 steam drifters, coming from the East Coast, every spring, engaged in it. The season started off the Wolf, in an area sometimes called 'the Silver Pits'. Following this fishing went deeper, to the west of Scilly in June and finally to the vicinity of Land's End, but when the hot weather came the mackerel was no longer a marketable fish in the conditions then obtaining. The East Coast drifters continued to come during the 1930s, but by 1939 the number of steam drifters in Newlyn was down from its peak of 200 to 24. The last four came in 1966. The failure of the mackeral and herring in the thirties contributed to a situation where concerts were held in aid of poor fishermen in Cornwall.

Forty years later in 1966–67 came a resurgence of mackerel, but in the form of a winter stock, previously unknown, or, some say, supposedly unknown. In the Cornish peninsula, with its small population, there was little capital available for the exploitation of this benefit. In terms of employment and the conservation of the stock this was a good thing. Apart from drift netting and occasionally seining, casual catches of mackerel had always been made with a single trailing spinner – 'whiffing', involving the use of a punt and oars. These were very small catches for local sale or merely an evening contribution to the pot by locals and visitors. In 1948 feathers were introduced from Scotland as a very effective way of catching mackerel, with fifteen on a line being jigged up and down from a small boat drifting with wind and tide. Moreover it was such a simple method of fishing that the investment in boat, gear and skill was minimal. In the classical world the Greeks were feared, even when they brought benefits, *Timeo Danaos et dona ferentes*. The same could have been said of the Scots in this instance. The Cornish accepted the gift of feathering, but later the Scots came south with their big purse-seiners and put an end to the inshore mackerel fishery on any large scale.

By the autumn of 1975 the herring had failed in the north and also British trawlers had been excluded from Icelandic waters following the 'cod wars', with the result that boats from Scotland, Fleetwood and Hull descended on the winter mackerel. The local boats counted their catches in stones, the purse-seiners and mid-water trawlers in tons. By February 1980 the boom was at an end. Most people would ascribe the decline in stocks, followed by close Ministry controls, to straight over-fishing, but it has been suggested that the winter stocks of mackerel were in any case a fluke of nature. More ingeniously it is suggested that when the oil spill from the Torrey Canyon disaster of 1967 off Scilly was treated with detergent and sank to the bottom it turned in two or three years to pure protein and this could have attracted and increased the shoals: well, perhaps.

The difference between the traditional mackerel driving and purse-seining is that while a drift net is shot and left in the hope, not always fulfilled, that the fish will swim into it the purse seine is shot around an observed shoal, gathered in and hauled. Cornish fishermen could have had them a century ago. An American purse seine, 200 fathoms in length was on show at the great Fisheries Exhibition of 1883. It was claimed that it could be shot around a shoal, pursed and the shoal caught in ten minutes – with luck. A catch of 80,000 fish had been made in such a way. The point was not missed by E. W. Crofts, writing in *The Cornishman* at the time, under the pen name of *Ouit*. 'We live in an age of quiet change and revolution, and our fishermen will no longer be able quietly to follow in the footsteps of their fathers and great-grandfathers. If they would hold their own in the competitive markets they must diligently study the time in which they live. The Fisheries Exhibition, now being held, will materially affect the interests of fishermen all the world over. The change in the mode of curing pilchards described last week is significant. The near future will be pregnant with innovations and inventions, and we already hear from several quarters of contemporary changes or modifications in the existing mode of fishery, and just to mention one thing, fishing with deep sea seans, as already practised by American fishermen, will probably be before long a fait accompli in Mount's Bay and other parts of Cornwall. It will never do for Cornish fishermen to hold blindly to the old ways: they must keep up with the revolutionary tide which is setting in, or come to grief.'.

Crofts' advice, sound on the face of it, was not taken, fortunately. He was obviously far-seeing, but not far-seeing enough to predict a run-down of stocks if methods became too efficient.

The pilchard fishery was perhaps the first to be severely affected by the advent of powered fishing craft. About the time of the First World War the pilchard shoals which had appeared close inshore at the end of July from time immemorial came no longer. The age-old seine-fishing industry of the ports and coves died. A number of fanciful reasons have been advanced for this but the simple fact is that probably the constant activity of the motor pilchard-drivers was breaking up the shoals further out. This had been a historic complaint against sailing drivers but in practice their effect had not been serious. The motor-drivers shot nets 80 yards in length, 30 to 40 yards deep, with between twenty and thirty of them to form a train.

However, the eventual extinction of the pilchard fishery came about not from over-fishing but through the complications of marketing, competition and changes in public taste. The driving season started at the Wolf in the autumn and worked up into Mount's Bay. In the 1950's the fleet, with its myriad deck lights, was like a small town at sea. Viewed from Penzance on a calm, clear October night the fleet made a line of lights along the horizon under the brilliant constellation of Orion, low in the sky. Later in the year the fishing moved towards Plymouth and went on in post-war years until January.

The exporting of fish from Cornwall goes back at least until the 13th century. Pilchards, preserved by pressing and salting, were popular in Italy for centuries and their export one of Newlyn's staples. But after 1918 this trade began to decline through a rather curious economic contradiction. The Italian economy was in a poor way and the country's exchange rate bad, until the United Kingdom came off the Gold Standard in 1931. This brought some revival, but the worsening political situation in Europe and Italy's invasion of Abyssinia contributed to a final decline in the trade. Another factor was the fact that salted fish were a traditional food of the poorer masses but as the economies of the Latin countries improved in the second half of the century the taste for it declined.

Technology, in any case, eventually overtook the long and laborious process of salting pilchards. The principle of 'sell what you can and can what you can't' was introduced in Cornwall as early as 1873, at Mevagissey. After 1945 there were a number of Cornish ports with canners, including Newlyn, but South Africa began to take the trade. Walvis Bay, in South-West Africa, began landing 500,000 tons of pilchards a year, at a shilling (5p) a stone to the fishermen, while 3/6 (17½) was being paid in Cornwall. A 70ft purse-seiner, in Walvis Bay, could catch 3,000 stone a day, equal to an average night's fishing for the entire Cornish fleet. At one time the African fishery was sending a bulk-carrier every other month to Avonmouth with 20,000 tons of pilchard meal alone. In the end Walvis Bay was fished out, but in the meantime the Cornish industry had virtually died. The Ministry of Agriculture and Fisheries investigated. It was established that there were stocks deep in the Channel through the year and that these could be viably fished with larger boats. The fishermen replied that, given the pilchards, catching was not the problem, but larger boats in their drying harbours would be an insoluble problem. And that was the end of that.

The migration patterns and feeding habits of pilchards are complex, but there is no need at the moment for an academic study of the pilchard shoals. Such influences as the decline in numbers of larval crabs or the possible effects of the sardine fishery further south would be important if there was a market for pilchards. Indeed there are pilchards still to be caught. Sometimes they are; but nobody wants them.

The demise of pilchard fishing was accompanied by the decline of long-lining, usually a summer occupation for the drivers. This method involved some six miles of line with 5,000 hooks, anchored to the bottom. Newlyn boats did three shots a trip and two trips a week. Even before the Second World War trawling had forced long-liners to go over a hundred miles out. It was an arduous form of fishing which did not damage the sea bed, but everything was against it. Pilchards for bait became scarce. Many of the species caught were not the most popular and only commanded low prices, such as ray, skate, conger and ling. The gear was vulnerable and it was claimed that trawling destroyed the grounds, so in time long-lining was replaced by gill-netting.

For a short time in the 1960's the long-liners turned to crabbing. The use of the term crabbing is itself of significance. The public generally speak of 'lobster pots', the fishermen of 'crab pots'. Lobsters have always been comparatively scarce but take the lead in British taste, with crab for sandwiches a long way second. The crayfish comes virtually nowhere. The Concise Oxford Dictionary defines the crayfish or crawfish first as a 'small freshwater crustacean' and only second as the marine spiny lobster. The remaining commercial species, the spider crab, has in the past been completely disregarded in this country by public and fishermen alike. On the other hand the Bretons and French have always had a high regard for the *langouste* (crayfish) and the spider crab. A certain amount of bartering with French crabbers for crayfish in exchange for lobsters used to go on offshore, with perhaps a little drop of something of which H.M. Customs would not have approved.

The shellfish trade is an important part of Newlyn's fishing but was not always so. In the sea off West Cornwall crabbing has been traditionally confined to the summer months. The ground swell and heavy seas of winter would destroy strings of pots and even summer gales can cause considerable damage. In Newlyn investment in boats went into those suitable and big enough for the mackerel and pilchard fishery, spanning most of the year. There was no point in investing in crabbers which could only work in the summer if there was a harbour from which boats could be working all the year around. Crabbing was left to the western coves like Penberth, Porthgwarra and Sennen. They had little choice. Conditions and facilities ruled out winter fishing and they had to exist on summer crabbing and summer and autumn seining for pilchards. Some of the Sennen men also went over to Scilly to fish every summer and this practice continued until after the Second World War. In the last century some Sennen men even went to St. Bride's Bay in West

Wales, and landed shellfish in Milford Haven. Considering that their heavily sparred and canvassed luggers were open boats and little over 21ft on the waterline this was a remarkable migration. There is not much in the way of havens on the coast of the North Channel until Milford is reached and a passage in such boats would not appeal to many today.

The men of the coves occupied the dead time of the year in making new pots for the next season. Sennen men cut withies from as far away as Marazion Marsh and 'The Withy Garden' under Sancreed Beacon. Such an activity would not appeal to fisherman in Newlyn who could go to sea for most of the year.

What the cove men could not do was provide their own marketing organisation. This was left to buyers in Newlyn who could despatch shellfish to destinations at home or abroad. They bought from the western coves and also from Cadgwith on the eastern side of the Lizard. Early in the field were W. Harvey & Sons, Josiah Pawlyn, Chivers, and Rogers, the last coming from Beesands in Devon. Originally shellfish were sold in single units in the case of crays and lobsters by the dozen in the case of crabs. However, a one pound lobster counted as only half a lobster. There was no processing of crabs and great difficulty in selling female crabs. The Ouhlen family of France purchased crays from Newlyn and Scilly. After 1945 they sent a carrier vessel, *Lutine* to Newlyn and continued to do so until 1970, when cross-channel road transport became more economical.

Between 1939 and 1945 the fishing grounds were rested, particularly from the attentions of French crabbers. Outside the three mile limit these sailing vessels, much larger than the Cornish open inshore boats had traditionally worked the South-West grounds and their presence was a feature of Newlyn life when they congregated in the harbour. At low water the crews would search for small bivalves for a meal; a prospect which did not appeal to locals with a knowledge of the sewage system. More healthily, a shop by what is now a Chinese restaurant in Street-an-Nowan used to bake French bread, which was sold by one Howard Badcock in flat cane baskets. When ashore the crews liked to stroll along to Penzance Promenade and the clack of their Breton sabots was a familiar sound. More spectacularly, thirty or forty crabbers would join in Marazion Regatta, in competition with Brixham trawlers, a splendid event of which a modern 'old gaffers' yacht rally can only be an echo. The author well remembers seeing three crabbers in line ahead running for Newlyn in a northerly gale. They had not shortened sail, as the wind was off-shore, and spray was bursting half way up their mainmasts. They presented a spectacle of working sailing vessels of a kind which will never be seen again.

Before the Second World War shellfish stocks were not a problem. The Cornish boats were small and were restricted to about seventy pots per man. Hauling was manual, easier with a little bit of sea running, as the hauler took up the slack smartly as the bow dipped. The petrol-paraffin engines would not idle satisfactorily to drive a small winch up forward and the small marine diesel was undeveloped. After the war methods were improved and the French began evolving motor crabbers. Cornish crabbers increased in size, the long-liners joined in, and then the skin divers arrived in the 1960's. Also the netting of crays revived as the modern nets did not suffer from the mending difficulties of cotton nets. The long-liners ravaged the grounds off Land's End, but the divers were another matter. Without the trouble and expense of making pots they simply plucked crayfish off the bottom. The traditional fishermen were neither inclined to follow the method nor tolerate it.

In the year 1966 it was estimated that divers were taking 40–45% of the catch. There were in fact only sixteen to twenty known professional divers but their effort was supplemented by an unknown number of amateurs, such as holiday makers and service personnel from the big air stations. With experience the divers worked all the grounds and stripped them from Newlyn to the Runnelstone, moving on to Land's End, St. Ives and Newquay. Negotiations to obtain an agreement between the fishermen and the divers appear to have failed as the divers would not accept a division of the grounds. Violence was forecast. The fisherman took to netting crays. In the end the problem seems to have solved itself by the temporary exhaustion of stocks.

Since then the industry has taken on a new shape. It was in 1966 that the British territorial limit was extended to six miles and this helped to reduce French competition. Small inshore boats still work and '*toppers*', or marker floats, may be seen all around the coast. Off-shore a 40ft boat may now set 350 pots. Harvey's *Julian Paul*, a 49 footer out of Newlyn is setting 640 pots. In terms of value the fishery has shown an enormous increase at Newlyn. Newlyn statistics are given in value at the date shown for the landings so that allowance must be made for inflation and the escalation in the real cost of shellfish to the buyer. In 1911 just £311 worth was landed. In 1950 the figure was £3,062. By 1970 it had increased to £38,120. By 1970 it had jumped to £202,741 and more than trebled by 1985 to £639,892. The inflation factor since 1950 is about 10, so that even allowing for some real increase in price the expansion has been enormous.

At sea metal pots are now the general rule, although some withy pots are still made in the district, and the boats are equipped with Decca navigators and efficient modern haulers. On shore the scene has changed. Originally floating vivier boxes moored in Newlyn harbour or at the back of the South Pier were used for storage, but the increasing use of the harbour brought more surface oil and W. Harvey & Sons built 20–30 ton capacity storage tanks on shore behind the South Pier, in 1979. This firm may now receive 7–10 tons of crabs and 2–3 tons of lobsters and crayfish per day. Some crabs are processed in Newlyn, some go to Billingsgate and other markets, others are cooked and vacuum packed for the Continent and Scandinavia. In fact the bulk of shellfish, especially spider crabs, go to the Continent.

At present there are some eighteen boats working out of Newlyn competing with other West Country crabbers and the French, who now have vessels carrying 1,000 pots. The pressure is on. A Newlyn skipper stated recently that ten years ago 200 pots would produce a good living, although the work was hard. Now 600 pots and an 80-hour week are needed for the same result. Over half the return can go in expenses and the escalation of the latter is not matched by increased prices in the market. And there is always the chance of gear being destroyed by foreign trawlers.

The inevitable question is whether there is over-fishing which will lead the present increase in trade to turn into a decline. The trade has declined before. The year 1933 was a peak pre-war one for the Cornish fishery. In 1947 even on the post-war rested grounds, catches only returned to half the 1933 figure, but that could be attributed to the drift away from crabbing as a seasonal occupation in the coves to steadier or easier work. Now the pressure is in the opposite direction. With unemployment at approaching 30% in West Cornwall, and even 50% in the mining parishes, enterprise in fishing has renewed attractions. Will more people be going after less fish on over-fished grounds? As with other species there is not much agreement on the factors which may affect the levels of stocks.

There is no doubt that crayfish stocks have been reduced. So much so in Scilly, for instance, that there has been a population explosion among the sea-urchins in the *lebensraum* created. But little is known about the breeding grounds of crayfish. It is known that they breed in groups and communicate by sound but the fact that no-one has ever caught one less than four inches long is held to confirm that their breeding activity takes place elsewhere, perhaps deep in the Atlantic. The fact that Scilly and Mount's Bay crayfish are generally smaller suggests that the new stock comes in from the south-west. But while the breeding grounds may be untouched fewer breeding stock may return to them each year. It has also been suggested that alterations in Atlantic sea-temperatures may have had an effect. In the past scientists have suggested that a decline in the phosphate and plankton content of the sea may have reduced the lobster population.

In 1986 the minimum regulation size for hen crabs was increased to 5½ ins., which had little effect as the markets had not accepted anything smaller for many years. But the increase in the minimum size for cock crabs to 6.3 ins. was held to cause a serious loss of earnings for inshore fishermen. The argument has been advanced that there should also be a maximum size regulation to protect the mature breeding stock.

Thus a number of traditional fisheries, once staples of Newlyn's economy have disappeared, seriously declined, or are under pressure. Although it should be noted that the decline of the fishery is not always exactly equated with the disappearance of stocks. Contrariwise the increase of a fishery is not necessarily equated with the appearance of new stocks, except perhaps in the case of mackerel. However, it would be quite wrong to assume that the importance of Newlyn has declined either absolutely or in relation to other ports, as the following statistical table on page 107 shows. Only the values of fish landed on first hand sale are available. Allowance has therefore to be made for inflation over a very long period, but relatively the figures, expressed in £s, tell their story.

Newlyn is said to be now the fourth largest port for fishing south of the Scottish border, exceeding Hull, North Shields, Lowestoft and Fleetwood in importance. About one seventh of the total national fish catch is now being taken off Devon and Cornwall. The fleet is the largest in the village's history. There are over twenty trawlers, ranging from 75ft to 90ft keel measurement and about twenty smaller trawlers ranging from 40ft to 60ft keel length. There are also over thirty netters ranging from 45ft to 55ft overall, eighteen shellfish boats and over forty small craft ranging down to punt size. About 750 are directly employed in the industry and many others in ancillary occupations.

The remarkable increase in the importance of Newlyn has come in the last twenty years or so, as the figures opposite indicate. The Newlyn Pier and Harbour Commissioners have responded accordingly.

Value of fish landed at Newlyn since 1910

	Mackerel £	Trawl and line £	Herring £	Pilchard £	Shell £	Total £
1910	80,511	19,606	2,040	7,070	311	109,548
1918	7,849	11,823	386	953	19	21,030
1920	208,018	37,204	8,848	20,049	268	274,387
1930	57,472	51,960	3,360	29,624	1,364	143,780
1940	28,447	111,592	9,860	5,931	1,089	156,919
1944	1	273,689	20	28,575	4,675	306,960
1950	49,841	173,071	216	19,309	3,062	245,499
1960	40,473	241,019	74	42,297	5,615	329,478
1970	62,821	282,766	0	6,125	38,120	389,832
1980	706,299	3,455,005	0	0	202,741	4,364,045
1984	344,112	6,739,314	0	0	639,892	7,723,318
1985–6 (Financial year)	86,612	9,365,330	0	0	332,113	9,784,055

Figures are by courtesy of the Newlyn Pier & Harbour Commissioners. Since 1950 the inflation factor in the monetary economy is reckoned to be of the order of 10.

The only surviving cobbled street in Newlyn, Chapel Street. (*Photo: Spectrum Studio*)

CHAPTER ELEVEN

Development And Destruction

The ways of the "delectable Duchy" have a rich complexity denied to the single-strand Englishman. To compare the crew of the Rosebud *to hunger marchers is to trample on romance. They are not asking for bread but for stones, the stones of their old homes.*

(*The Times* October 23rd, 1937)

There is a bewildering variety of port and harbour administrations in Britain. They include public companies, private companies, public trusts, local government, public trusts turned public companies, nationalised authorities turned public company and Harbour Commissioners. The last are a statutory body set up under the provisions of an Act of Parliament, the original Act being the General Pier and Harbour Act of 1861. It would perhaps be an exaggeration to call its provisions for Commissioners an early kind of nationalisation under a Liberal government, but it provided for the appointment by the Board of Trade of representatives of the various interested parties.

There was amending legislation in 1884 and at that time the Commissioners appointed for Newlyn were no less than twenty-three in number to run the harbour still in the course of completion. An Act of 1906 reduced the body to the more manageable number of nine, representing the boat-owners, the Board of Trade, the Cornwall County Council. There were some interesting provisions in the original powers including a limit on the number of houses of the 'Labouring Classes' which might be acquired, with an elaborate definition of those classes. Some now outdated items in the dues list were black jack (per ton), brimstone (per cwt.) chairs, common (per doz.), slates (writing), ice, spermaceti and paintings. The last were charged at 3d (1p) per foot, which may have been of some interest to the Newlyn School of Artists.

Once the final new harbour works had been completed at the beginning of the century no major decisions faced the

Commissioners until the second half of the century. When the maximum length of boat was only a little over 50ft, drying out alongside served, or was made to serve, for repairs and re-fits. The increasing size of the trawlers demanded something better and accordingly a heave-up slip, with cradle, was built, capable of taking vessels up to 100ft keel length and 24ft beam.

Apart from the slip there was no significant development of harbour facilities until the late 1970s, but the fishing fleet had been developing both in numbers and in the size of vessels involved. The greatest change was in the growth of trawl fishing. To the traditional Newlyn fisherman, brought up in a world of long-liners and drift net boats, mainly family owned, trawling was still a dirty word. Brixham sailing trawlers had never been popular, because it was believed they damaged the breeding grounds and paid scant attention to the presence of drift nets in their path and power trawlers in their turn represented even more of a threat. However the decline of pilchard driving and long-lining left a vacuum which trawler owners, principally W. Stevenson & Sons, began to fill.

The Stevenson family firm began when James Harvey, a Great Yarmouth fish merchant, came to Newlyn in the 1850's and married Elizabeth Johns, who ran her own pilchard curing business. They built Norfolk House on the Old Quay slipway. Harvey died at an early age but his widow became the first independent producer to enter into the pilchard export trade. Her contemporary William Stevenson owned two luggers, *W & J*, PZ78 and *Excellent*, PZ513. (There is still an *Excellent*, PZ513 in the Stevenson fleet.) William died in 1874 and his son William took over as skipper of the *Excellent* at the age of 18 and in 1889 he married Sara Ann, a daughter of the widow Harvey. In 1894 Stevenson sold his boats and joined his mother-in-law in business and the firm continued to trade under the name of Stevenson & Harvey after her death in 1900. William Stevenson's four sons joined him in the business in the 1920s, and expanded to include fish selling, baking and grocery interests. In the 1930's the firm went back into boat owning with the purchase of the 80ft M.V.F. *Efficient* (later *Excellent*) and the 65ft M.F.V.'s *Trevessa* and *Madeline*). By the 1950s Stevenson's had seventeen side-winder trawlers, but in 1974 they carried out the first conversion in the U.K. to beam trawling with the 92ft *Elizabeth Ann Webster*.

Sailing trawlers had always used a single beam trawl on the port side, hauled by a warp forward with power from a steam capstan. With the introduction of power propulsion, providing constant way on the vessel, otter boards were substituted to keep the mouth of the trawl open, but now in its turn this method has been superseded by heavy beam trawls slung from each side of the vessel by derricks. In 1976 Stevenson's acquired the first of seven Dutch beamers. There are now over twenty large trawlers in the Stevenson fleet and the firm is solely owned and run by the brothers Tony and William Stevenson and their sister Mrs Jacqueline Webster. There are three other large trawlers operated by other owners in the port, but Stevenson's can now claim to have the largest owner fleet of trawlers in the British Isles. The sphere of operation is from 100 miles off the Start, around to the Western Approaches and north to Lundy, including the Labadie Bank, Great Sole Bank, Little Sole Bank, Jones' Bank and other grounds. The large trawler fleet of vessels with 75–90ft keel length is supplemented by an almost equal number of boats with 40–60ft keel length, including pair and mid-water trawlers.

The contribution of trawling to the Newlyn fishery of the trawlers can be seen from the statistical table on page 107. The trawl and line column needs some interpretation. With the decline of long lining it can be taken that the figures from 1970 onwards relate to trawling for the most part. The figures for 1940 and 1944 are much higher than might be expected, given that most of the fishermen were serving in the Royal Navy. The explanation lies in the presence of a large Belgian, French and Dutch refugee trawler fleet which operated throughout the war, some of the French to the distant waters of the Grand Banks. However, the presence of foreign trawlers is also a peacetime event. Newlyn is a statutory harbour of refuge. Apart from southern Irish ports it is the nearest and best refuge for fishing vessels in the Western Approaches. In bad weather French boats appear and in very bad weather, particularly outside the winter season, the big Belgian and Dutch beamers come for shelter. On one day in April 1983 there were tiers of large trawlers along the North Pier up to eight deep.

This occasional demand, added to the increasing number of local trawlers and the new generation of 40ft class netters led to a major decision to increase the quay space within the existing harbour. The scheme involved building a new pier about 250ft to the south-west of the North Pier and parallel to it. It was intended to be 1,000ft in length, but shortage of capital and grants reduced it to 750ft. On the south-west side its length is reduced to 300ft by the infill which has created a large lorry park and car park for the use of fishermen and port users. The park also accommodates a small assembly building constructed by the R.N.L.I. for the lifeboat berth which lies off the pier. The work started in February 1979 and involved the dredging of 120,000 cubic metres of spoil to obtain a depth of 2.25 metres below Low Water Ordinary Spring Tides. To form the batter along the edge of the car park and lorry park area 15,000 tonnes of rock were dumped. The new Mary Williams pier was completed for £1,472,000 and the first landings took place in the early summer of 1980. It was officially opened by The Queen on the 28th of November in that year and has been heavily used ever since.

Not long after the new development at Newlyn the auld enemy, Penzance, decided again to offer competition to Newlyn. Although it is not really fair to say 'Penzance', the borough council having come to an end in 1974. Local government re-organisation replaced it with Penwith District Council which decided, very sensibly, that something would have to be done with the deteriorating Rank building at the harbour, built for coastal flour imports in the thirties. It was a choice of demolition or conversion and they chose the latter course at a cost of about £90,000. Unfortunately they also decided that it would make a good fish market. Newlyn thought otherwise, and said so, in no uncertain terms. Early in 1986 the venture collapsed, with debts owing to the council and amid a chorus of 'Told you so!' from Newlyn.

In the meantime Newlyn was nurturing plans for a 300ft extension to the now paid-for Mary Williams pier. The expenditure of another £1½ million will include the enlarging and modernisation of the fish market, with a new 22ft roadway outside it linking the North Pier and the Mary Williams pier. Extensive dredging will enable boats to come alongside the market at most states of tide. The scheme awaits sufficient Government and EEC grant aid.

The face of Newlyn has been much changed in the course of the last century. Not least among the waterfront developments have been the premises of Sutton's and Shippam's devoted to fish processing and the major expansion of the ice works. This enterprise superseded the import of natural ice from Norway in 1908. The business, now owned by W. Stevenson & Sons was founded in 1908 by R. R. Bath, a clever fisherman from a Devon family. A well sunk on the spot was contaminated with iron and the then large sum of £3,000 was spent in piping water from Sheffield, in Paul parish, a mile and a quarter away.

The industrial changes in Newlyn have, inevitably, been accompanied by social and domestic change, although fortunately much of the fabric of the old village has survived, in the face of many short sighted attempts to destroy it.

There remain two places in Newlyn which look like bomb sites, but they are not the work of the *Luftwaffe*, even though that air force dropped 400 bombs in the Penzance area and killed over twenty people. They were created by Penzance Town Council in a wave of demolition which was only stayed by the advent of the Second World War. One of the largest sites was not put into use (as the inevitable car park) until some forty years had elapsed.

The trouble began in 1934 when the borough of Penzance was extended to take in Newlyn, Paul, Mousehole and part of Gulval. The enlarged council had the duty of implementing the Housing Acts and in the unvarnished term then used this meant 'slum clearance'. An area adjacent to the harbour in Penzance was cleared and replaced by the unlovely Penalverne estate, and the council then turned its attention to the 'slums' of Newlyn. There was indeed a good deal of sub-standard housing, crowded and insanitary, but there was also a great number of houses, solidly built of granite, which are sound homes today and with proper maintenance will be there on Judgement Day. However, the Council proposed to clear most of Newlyn Town from North Corner southward and then to start on Street-an-Nowan. Mousehole was to come later.

In place of Newlyn town a new estate was to be built at the top of Chywoone Hill. That this involved fishermen climbing a 1:5 hill to homes with no storage space for their gear, and the old and infirm living cut off from shops and social facilities did not enter the council's thinking. Moreover it was proposed that the owners of houses covered pink on the plans would receive site value and those in the grey areas the market value. Some of these homes had been bought with the savings of two generations, contained cellars and

Duke Street in the Street-an-Nowan part of Newlyn, showing on the left a typical house with the living accommodation above and a fish cellar below, with old hogsheads in the foreground. This part of Newlyn was demolished c. 1937. (*Photo: Reg Watkiss collection*)

net lofts and were all adjacent to the harbour. The compensation would be minimal, as little as £12.6s.8d (£12.36p) in some cases. The new location would be a burden, while the rent to be paid would soon eat up the compensation.

Newlyn reacted to the proposals in a strong and determined manner. The people were quite capable of speaking for themselves locally, but national backing for their cause was another matter. At this point the Newlyn artists joined the cause. The Newlyn School of artists had begun to gather strength in the previous century when Stanhope Forbes formed them into a Society about 1884. At that time they were *avant-garde* post-Impressionist and had adopted the French *plein-air* style of painting. Broadly speaking this meant taking their canvases on site rather than creating in the studio. By degrees they became accepted and integrated into the community, particularly in the second generation, although they did to some extent fuel the move towards de-industrialisation in taking over net lofts and fishermen's dwellings. It is the first sign we have of arts and crafts beginning to replace basic industry in Cornwall. In 1890 Thomas Bedford Bolitho, ever mindful of the people's welfare, started the Newlyn Industrial Class. Under J. D. Mackenzie and others, young fishermen were taught an alternative skill which is commemorated in Newlyn copperware. In 1920 the Crysede Company was started in Sambo's Row on St. Peter's Hill and flourished in silk printing and design, bringing more industrial craft work to the village.

One of the most prominent artists was Thomas Cooper Gotch, who lived at Wheal Betsy. His daughter, Phyllis Maureen, the Marquise de Verdières, with others formed the Newlyn & District Housing Advisory Committee. The Chairman was Geoffrey Garnier, a Lancashire man and an engineer, who had turned to art and become a brilliant engraver, distinguished for his aquatints. The Committee did more than draw local attention to the plight of those suffering from the insensitive attitude of the Council. They engaged the services of S. D. Adshead, Emeritus Professor of Town Planning at the University of London. He pointed out that, while some houses would have to go, the council's scheme did not have to be either a clearance order or an improvement order, but could be a combination of the two. However, despite a public inquiry the council did not accept this. Perfectly sound houses were condemned merely for lack of indoor sanitation and even half a century ago the local authority was under the spell of the motor car, as part of the scheme was to drive an improved road through Newlyn so that traffic could speed through the village to go no further than Mousehole.

The controversy involving wholesale demolition in a picturesque Cornish fishing village began to attract the attention of news desks in Fleet Street. The Marquise de Verdières, Secretary of the Advisory Committee, was a persuasive leader with a gift for publicity and capable of charming her way through bureaucratic thickets. She, with others, devised a masterpiece of public relations for the cause, which combined maximum 'grass roots' involvement with maximum national publicity. Possibly inspired by the famous Jarrow March of 1936 they planned a deputation to London, but no ordinary one. They would send a crew of Newlyn fishermen, in their normal rig, in a Newlyn boat to Westminster Pier to present a petition to the Minister of Housing in the Palace of Westminster. Today such an event would attract only passing attention, as did the Cornish miners march through London in January 1986. In the thirties it was an original and brilliant stroke. The boat selected was the long-liner/pilchard driver *Rosebud*, PZ87. The crew were led by Cecil Richards, a man of distinguished intellect and traditional Methodist piety, who later became Sea Fisheries Officer for Cornwall County Council.

The *Rosebud* was built in Newlyn in 1919 for the brothers Cecil and Willy Richards and was the pride and joy of her builder, Joe Peake. At dawn on October 20th, 1937 she left Newlyn for the 450-mile passage to the Thames. On board were Cecil Richards, Willy Richards, J. S. Matthews, J. R. Harvey ('Sailor Joe'), J. H. Tonkin, W. H. Williams, J. Simons, B. G. Batten and W. Roberts. With them they carried a petition for their homes signed by 1,093 people, together with such local offerings for Godspeed as a bottle of Jordan water and a bottle of water from Madron Well. On October 22nd they arrived at Westminster Pier to meet the Minister, Sir Kingsley Wood, for tea in the House. The visit soon passed into legend. Wives and supporters travelled to London by train to join the men and press and newsreel coverage went nationwide. Sir Kingsley was a smooth politician and besides providing Cornish cream for tea laid on the diplomatic manner fairly thickly. But at least one of the crew was not to be outdone. 'Sailor Joe' bade him farewell as a 'friend not a Minister'. Sir Kingsley replied: 'You should have been the diplomat and I should have been the fisherman'. In the event Sir Kingsley proved to be a Minister and not a friend. When his decision arrived Cecil Richards sagely observed: 'As a fisherman I know there is a big difference between seeing a shoal of fish in the sea and actually getting it in the net. I am inclined to think now that we have not much to rejoice about in this decision.' Of the 157 properties in the Order, only 23 were excluded altogether, 54 owners were given market value, and 17 received payment for 'well maintained houses'. A large part of The Backside was demolished, with St. Peter's Square and part of St. Peter's Hill. The inhabitants were removed to the airy heights of the Gwavas Estate, whether they liked it or not. Newlyn being a Celtic community there had of course been division within. It took the shape of a counter-petition by those, chiefly tenants and younger folk who welcomed the idea of going to modern accommodation.

In the next two years further pressure on Penzance town council brought some change in their policy, but the strongest influence was the outbreak of war in September 1939. Many of the condemned houses were then filled with refugee families from the Continent and since then the lower part of Newlyn Town has changed but little, apart from the tidying up and surfacing of most, but not all, of the St. Peter's Square area. By Time's irony Newlyn, including the further parts the council wished originally to clear, is now a Conservation Area!

The social changes have been greater than the structural ones. Whereas half a century ago almost everyone in Newlyn belonged to a family involved in the fishing industry, directly or indirectly, or would be associated with some other local industry, Newlyn is now socially in the main a suburb of Penzance. Many fishermen now live in various parts of Penzance.

Employment in Newlyn in industries not related to fishing has also declined. In 1896 the Consolidated Tin Smelting Co.'s works at Trereife, in Newlyn Combe, closed during an earlier crisis decade in Cornish mining. The Sanatogen Works took their place and later a fish meal factory. The site has now been re-developed for small industries. Penlee Quarry is not actually at Penlee Point, but close to Newlyn Town. The rock is basic igneous greenstone, known locally, rather confusingly, as 'blue elvan'. The rock is as hard as cast-iron and finds a home and Continental market as roadstone. Work began to develop early in the century and in the 1930's about 300 men were employed. Many walked to and fro from Penzance and wielded a 28lb sledgehammer all day. In 1945/46 exports from the South Pier at Newlyn were 88,617 tons. In 1958/59 granite from Castle-an-Dinas Quarry was added and export tonnage peaked at 551,012 tons in 1973/74. In 1981/82 Castle-an-Dinas closed and tonnage fell sharply. In 1984/85 it was down to 76,100 tons, which was less than the 1945/46 figure, but in 1985/86 it rose again to 106,000 tons. Blue elvan is so hard that it is only used for sub-bases on U.K. roads.

The dues levied in connection with stone exports and miscellaneous vessels and yachts are a contribution to the harbour's income, but fishing and related industries are the base of the port's economy as much as ever they were. But the future of the fishing industry is the subject of many doubts and fears. How secure is the future?

The long liner/pilchard driver *Rosebud PZ 87*, which took Newlyn's petition against Penzance Town Council's demolition programme to Westminster Pier in October 1937. A plaque commemorating this event has been placed on the wall of the Royal National Mission to Deep Sea Fishermen by the Newlyn Association and was unveiled on October 20th, 1987, the fiftieth anniversary of the *Rosebud*'s sailing. (*Photo: Richards Collection, The Penzance Library.*

Part of the Newlyn fishing fleet in harbour in a winter gale of 1987. In the foreground is the old Medieval harbour. In the middle ground a mass of tiers of boats clustered around the new Mary Williams pier. Further away again is the inner part of the North Pier. (*Photo: John Corin*)

CHAPTER TWELVE

Conservation And Conflict

It is to be hoped the progress of ichthyology, and the art of fish-breeding, with our advancing knowledge of the habits of fish, may increase the supply.
(W. S. Lach-Szyrma, 1878)

Over ninety years on from the completion of its 19th century harbour scheme, with another quay added and to be further extended, it would be comforting to feel that Newlyn was set on a prosperous path for the remainder of this century and on into the next without too many worries about outside pressures. On the face of it Newlyn is flourishing as a fishing port, with fourth place in the U.K. in the value of catches landed and one of the four significant commercial ports in Cornwall.

Despite the summer tourist 'monsoon' which bursts over the county, Newlyn is resistant to de-industrialisation. Its old rival, St. Ives, is sadly a ghost port as far as fishing is concerned. The smell of fresh fish has been replaced by the unattractive reek of fish and chips. St. Ives, with the advantage of a closer rail connection than Newlyn, succeeded in discouraging Sunday fishers from the East Coast where Newlyn failed and paid a penalty in development in the long run. But basically its harbour suffers from a run of sea in bad weather and does not have Newlyn's space or facilities, so that to some extent decline was inevitable and the town embraced the tourist trade.

Tourism has become something of a sacred cow in Cornwall where nothing must be done which might offend the eyes of the summer visitor who is enraged by the sight of an oil-rig anchored in a bay. Meanwhile officially approved vandalism destroys countryside and townscapes. Penzance town council may be accused of starting it all when in 1866 they tried to ban Newlyn fishermen from bringing their boats to the Promenade beach and drying their nets, lest the practice should upset the visitors. The town council and the hoteliers were really alarmed in 1898 when a railway to Newlyn and

St. Just was proposed, which would have passed along the Promenade. The Railway Commissioners rejected the scheme.

In 1897 the proposal to build the Headland Hotel in Newquay and enclose traditional net drying grounds aroused fury among fishermen and other residents who were opposed to the tourist trade. There were threats, violence and riots, but in the end the hotel was built. Commenting on the tourist trade and its effect on Cornwall, Sir Arthur Quiller-Couch wrote in 1930: 'It is unhappily certain that any people which lays itself out to exploit the stranger and the tourist runs grave risk of deterioration in manliness; and as I had rather be poor myself than subservient, so I would rather see my countrymen poor than subservient.' At the present high level of tourist trade and high level of unemployment, along with low wages, in Cornwall Sir Arthur's countrymen may be both poor and subservient. The son of a Geevor miner recently put it more pithily. He wanted to become a miner, not a seller of ice-cream for a few months in the summer.

So far the strength of the fishing industry has resisted pressures from within Britain and not much happens in Newlyn to impede it. If visitors' cars are held up by congestion around the fish market they have to put up with it. On the other hand a threat has been discerned to the beauty of Newlyn Coombe in the shape of a possible development in connection with the planned Penzance distributor road, in itself a bitterly opposed project.

Newlyn is currently far more at risk from influences outside the United Kingdom. The competition for fish stocks from other countries in the European Economic Community is the main and continuing problem, coupled with increased efficiency of fishing methods. To-day we are very aware of the conflict between efficiency and conservation. The first signs of this conflict appeared a century ago. In 1866 the great naturalist T. H. Huxley had said that major fish stocks were inexhaustible. In the context of the fishing methods of the time he was possibly right. By 1881 another expert observer named de Caux had a different view: 'The stern fact is that the sea is exhaustible; and believing, as I do, that the great fish farm around the British Isles should be worked with judgement as well as with skill, I invite attention to these matters.' His use of the term 'farm' is misleading in so far as fish farming in the sea on any significant scale is something which has yet to happen. The fisherman is a hunter, raiding the fish stocks on the plains of the sea. In farming terms he reaps but does not sow, or to be more exact, kills but does not breed replacement stock. Moreover Huxley himself pointed out that it is useless just to protect the spawn and the fry. If you fish the mature fish too hard there will eventually be no spawn to protect. The year 1883, when the great International Fisheries Exhibition was staged, marked the beginning of new thought about exploitation and conservation. A Royal Commission was hearing that some stocks of trawled fish were showing a decline and the influential Exhibition was followed in the next year by the establishment of the Marine Biological Association, under the leadership of Huxley. The first laboratory of the Association was built on Plymouth Hoe, where it is still in operation.

Cornish and Scottish fishermen were, by reason of their smaller localised organisation with limited capital resources, conservationist in practice and outlook. The Cornish fisherman's organisation of and attitude to the industry remains in some respects steadfastly that of his great-grandfather, with small capital, small boats and unintensive fishing. Even their largest trawlers are not very large by international standards and Cornishmen will often contend that the larger boats with their high gross earnings and high costs gain little for the fishermen in terms of net profit. Moreover, many look on fishing not just as a means of income but as a way of life.

Not long ago a director of the Scottish Fishermen's Organisation wrote to *Fishing News* imputing greed to high gross earners and arguing that despite all their complaints they earn more than is required for a satisfactory life-style. Certainly when a man puts to sea in the face of Force 10–11 forecast to fish in the calm 'eye' of the depression in order to land fish when landings are very low, his conduct must be questioned.

Scotland, which did such damage to the mackerel stocks of the South West, seems to have been more favoured than the rest of Britain for the modernisation of its fishing fleet. According to recent figures 67% of the fleet south of the Border is over twenty years old, but only 34% in Scotland. However, the Government does not reckon to neglect the industry. In 1982, Peter Walker, then the Minister of Agriculture and Fisheries, said: 'This government's objective is to see that this component of the economy, a component managed by men of courage, independence and enterprise, will in future, be an expanding element of the British economy and not a contracting one.' Fine words.

One of the principal reasons why Norway opted to stay out of the E.E.C., if not the main reason, was the threat it saw in a Common Fisheries Policy, C.F.P. As far as Cornish fishermen are concerned the French, and to a lesser extent the Belgians, have always been seen as dangerous competitors and not very conservation minded. The admission of Spain to the EEC poses an even greater threat. It has not been forgotten that in 1595 Spanish raiders landed and burnt Paul, Penzance and Newlyn, including Paul Church. Blackened pillars in part of the Church are an ever-present reminder of this event. Some years ago a large sum was required for roof repairs in the church and the Parochial Church Council thought it very reasonable to write to the Spanish Ambassador for a contribution by way of reparation. In a letter full of courtly Spanish grace the Ambassador sent £50 and a gentle hint to the effect that Drake and his merry men had done a fair amount of damage to Spanish churches in their time and any reciprocal gesture would be most welcome. But the threat from Spain is now in essence dietary rather than ecclesiastical. In the past the taste for fish in Roman Catholic countries benefited Newlyn and indeed still does in that the bulk of fish landed in Newlyn is shipped to the Continent.

Spaniards eat several times more fish per head than the British and have a fishing fleet to match the demand which is why their entry into the E.E.C. and the C.F.P. was viewed with apprehension. The result has been bitter complaints about their disregard of quotas and regulations, accompanied by numerous arrests of their vessels. Newlyn regards the operation of fifty Spanish vessels under the British flag as a scandal. Of the sixteen vessels of the Fishery Protection squadron, four are deployed in the Western Approaches, along with aerial surveillance, but, as the Chief Inspector of Fisheries has commented, policing can never be a complete answer. There must be co-operation between fishermen as well.

A century ago Lach-Szyrma said that no man claimed an acre of ocean as his own. Despite the existence of exclusion zones, the extension of fishing limits, 'mackerel boxes', the introduction of quotas and various kinds of surveillance this remains true and certainly no one fishing port has the exclusive right to an acre of ocean. The outlook is subject to agreements, or disagreements, between both fishermen and nations. The advance of technology ensures that fish can be located and caught with terrifying efficiency. A modern device can identify a single cod at 1,500ft from a fishing vessel steaming at 17 knots.

Lach-Szyrma had a vision far ahead of his time, of an international effort by both black and white races to pursue the harvest of the sea, where he postulated an acre of sea would yield more food than an acre of land. Newlyn's remarkable Vicar would hardly be satisfied with the situation to-day. The sanctity of the Sabbath may no longer be an issue, but the pressures which caused the Newlyn men to riot a century ago are still never very far away.

Arguments about fishing have gone on as long as man has pursued the harvest of the sea but perchance the reader is weary of them and I would be wise to echo Carew's words as he drew to the end of his section on fishing in the famous *Survey of Cornwall*: 'But you are tired, the day is spent, and it is high time that I draw to harbour.'

Select Bibliography

Aflalo, F. G. *The Sea-Fishing Industry of England and Wales.* (Edward Stanford, 1904).

Batten, Ben *Newlyn Boyhood, Newlyn of Yesterday, Newlyn Heritage.* (Privately published).

March, Edgar J. *The Sailing Drifters.* (Percival Marshall, reprinted David & Charles 1970).

Pender, John J. *A Mousehole Man's Story.* (Privately published).

Pool, P. A. S. *History of the Town and Borough of Penzance* (The Corporation of Penzance):

Various *Lectures on Fishes, Fishing etc. Cornwall Fisheries Exhibition.* (Cornwall County Council, 1903).

Newspapers

The Cornishman
The Cornish Telegraph
Royal Cornwall Gazette
Western Morning News
West Briton

Three volumes of press cuttings re the *Rosebud* voyage collected by G. Garnier

Periodical

Peninsula Voice

Unpublished Memoirs

Brown, Blanche
Kelynack, Janie
Williams, William *Journal 1782–1836*
Worth,John T.

Index

General